BEYON

Hidden Truth about Reincarnation

ISABELLA A. GREENE

BEYOND THE TRAP

Hidden Truth About Reincarnation

Copyright © 2024 Isabella A. Greene

Cover Art: Facusio Creations
Editing: BookBright Co.

For those in the know

Contents

A Word from the Author

This book is the continuation of my first book, "LEAVING THE TRAP." It refers to it and builds upon it. I encourage you to read "LEAVING THE TRAP: How to Exit the Reincarnation Cycle" first, as without it, this book will appear incomplete or even confusing.

Lots of new insights came pouring into my awareness throughout the year that followed the publishing of "LEAVING THE TRAP." Weekly interviews, discussions, workshops, and a flood of questions that followed had me researching and wondering about things I had never questioned or was aware of before.

As I became strongly focused on the subject of reincarnation and the false narratives about it that are pressed into our minds from all directions, a new understanding of the way things are opened up to me.

These false narratives span from the traditional teachings of Eastern Religions to the present-day teachings of the "New Age" community. I am fully aware of how deeply the false beliefs that serve the cycle of reincarnation and the Matrix system are ingrained in our minds by now, as I myself was no exception. I invite you to put these beliefs on hold while you read what I have to offer you in this book. In order to discover the truth that works for you, I encourage you to read with an open mind and to dive into your own research and exploration, but mainly to put an effort into having your own non-physical experiences.

Volumes of words mean nothing compared to what you learn through just one or two of these experiences, let alone through multiple ones.

I am continuing to learn as time goes by, just like you. In this book, I intend to provide all of the information and recommendations I am currently aware of to assist you in sending your research in the right direction.

Ahead of you is the continuation of my story of venturing beyond the veil, along with techniques, new information, discoveries, questions, answers, and conclusions that I gathered since publishing "LEAVING THE TRAP."

Yours truly,

Isabella A. Greene

FOREWORD
How to Really Exit Reincarnation

My technique recommendations and tactics for exiting reincarnation are listed in my first book "LEAVING THE TRAP: How to Exit the Reincarnation Cycle."

The purpose of this book is mostly to delve deeper into the concepts I touched upon in "LEAVING THE TRAP" and to expand on the techniques mentioned in my first book, specifically The Cosmic Cobra Breath and the mid-sleep meditation.

This material is for those who are already "in the know" about the hidden aspects of the Matrix system we live in and for those who are ready to truly train for their final exit, not just gamble with it.

Practicing Cosmic Cobra Breath coupled with mid-sleep meditation every night, learning to facilitate out-of-body experiences by will, and then training yourself to quantum travel out of the dimensions of the Matrix while still alive is the only way that I know of today that assures your exit from the cycle of rebirth is successful.

In my opinion, this method guarantees your ability to bypass the entire entrapment mechanism and avoid the tunnel of white light, the handlers, and the afterlife dimension.

Additional recommendations in preparation for exiting the reincarnation cycle and learning how to handle your non-physical self and quantum travel out of the structure are to revoke all soul agreements and do the inner work to lighten your energetic load.

You can see the entire list of my recommendations and read about handling the interactions with the Archons in my book "LEAVING THE TRAP."

However, I now posit that *the entrapment escape happens right at the moment of passing*. If you missed your chance, went through the tunnel of light, and are facing the handlers, doing anything at that point, no matter how strong and ready you think you are to face them, is too late, and you are already trapped.

If all of what I mention above isn't sufficient for you, please feel free to visit my online school, The Void Academy, at www.TheVoidAcademy.net.

CHAPTER ONE
5D. Dimensions of the Matrix

PART ONE
Dimensions of the Matrix

Is reincarnation a part of the Matrix system?

Yes, most definitely. One fits the other like a glove. They are part of the same structure; they sustain and feed off of each other.

If the information about the Matrix system interests you, I recommend the brilliant works of David Icke, who explains the entire structure in great detail.

I didn't read anything between 2014, when I first started entering the quantum field of information and 2023 so, truth be told, I haven't read any of David Icke's books so far, but I became aware of the depth of his material through numerous video programs and discussions that filled my year.

That year, I was drawn to learn more about the yogic practices that lead to experiences of super-consciousness, so I read "The Yoga Sutras of Patanjali" and "Autobiography of a Yogi," written by the great yogic master Paramahansa Yogananda. These are the books that I also most highly recommend.

Even though Yogananda's book talks about the planets of the astral plane that are clearly part of the reincarnation system with all its "Karmic" laws, as the desirable afterlife destination, if you read with this awareness in mind, his book provides quite a glimpse into the layers of soul entrapment within the afterlife dimension.

Although the Matrix structure is not the prime objective of my book, let's quickly examine the key points about the Matrix.

What are the main characteristics and objectives of the system controlling and operating on this planet? It appears to be to utilize its subjects for the system's benefit, in complete disregard of its subjects' well-being.

And isn't the reincarnation cycle's main characteristic and objective exactly the same?

Both the Matrix system and the reincarnation cycle appear to operate within the same dimensional structure, aka "levels of consciousness," of planets, planes, worlds, and even universes where the above-mentioned objective is acceptable and the norm.

We live in 3D, and in "LEAVING THE TRAP," I wrote that the astral plane around Earth, where the reincarnation cycle is set up, stretches up to 4.9D.

Yet new awareness has emerged since then, and now I posit that both the Matrix and the reincarnation systems, without a doubt, also include the fifth dimension.

This is hard to admit due to our New Age attachment to the idea of the fifth dimension being the dimension of salvation. The attainment of the fifth-dimensional state of being is presented as highly desirable and the answer to all human concerns.

Like others within the New Age community, I too, was influenced by the false belief that the fifth dimension was outside the Matrix and the reincarnation system. Yet all along, I just couldn't shake the feeling of it not being entirely correct.

If the Matrix operates within the levels of consciousness where using its subjects for its own benefit is the way of being, then how does 5D fit into it?

Let's examine the beliefs about the fifth dimension that are currently in place within the New Age community.

It is believed that 5D provides emotional and material well-being, that all of our human problems vanish, and that we live within a reality closely resembling "Heaven on Earth."

What we are told to envision as the fifth-dimensional reality is the almost exact representation of the upper astral dimension, the heavenly realm that is part of the afterlife and the reincarnation cycle.

The only difference is that we are supposed to still be in the physical and have our physical desires fulfilled.

Both the Matrix and the reincarnation cycle utilize the hook of human desires to keep their subjects recycled and enslaved.

The fifth dimension, as we know it, and the very longing to get there, is all about the fulfillment of desires, and this appears to me to be part of the exact same mechanism as the entrapment system itself, except perhaps a bit better disguised.

The narrative is very much the same too: "Be this way and that way, and you will go to Heaven." "Be this way and that way, and you will live in the fifth dimension on Earth where all your wishes will come true."

All traditional Eastern teachings that point the way out of the entrapment of the souls from the cycles of "Maya" and "Samsara" (aka "the Matrix system") indicate that the freedom we are seeking lies beyond the influence of earthly desires.

The ultimate freedom of the liberated human comes from the level of elevated consciousness no longer attached to the idea of having their earthly desires fulfilled.

For more on this subject, I recommend reading the timeless classics such as "The Yoga Sutras of Patanjali" and also "Tao Te Ching" by Lao-Tzu.

PART TWO
5D and the Hooks of Earthly Desires

Earthly desires and the futile attempts to fulfill these desires are the hooks that keep human subjects within the Matrix. This is how the system feeds and sustains itself, utilizing our time, attention, and very life-force.

Disconnected from the awareness of our true higher essence, we spend our lives chasing the contentment that is promised through the fulfillment of earthly desires. Yet, for an average human being, this never occurs; it causes great suffering and carries over from one incarnation to the next.

Moreover, the promise of fulfilling desires is utilized by the handlers of the reincarnation cycle as a big carrot in the sky to lure us back into yet another lifetime on Earth.

Even if you are one of those few born into having everything provided for them materially—something less fortunate individuals spend their lifetimes chasing after—the desired fulfillment is never there.

The potential for earthly desires is endless and ever evolving. As long as we are within the Matrix system, there is always something else that our ego is after, be it a new house, a better job, the love of our life, achieving what's promised in spiritual teachings, or bringing ourselves into 5D, which holds the promise of fulfilling all our desires at once.

Is this 5D state of being possible while still alive? Yes, it is, but unfortunately, it does not liberate us from the Matrix system. I simply do not see a way to exit the Matrix system while living within it.

All of the present-day teachings about going off-grid and not utilizing anything the Matrix hooks us into only work to a certain degree; even fully disengaged, we still remain within the bubble of the Earth's Matrix system. As long as we are on Earth, we are living within the Matrix system, and there is no way around it.

The only tangible way out of the Matrix trap that I presently see is exiting the reincarnation cycle after passing. This allows us to escape from the system in its entirety.

Although we cannot escape the Matrix while still living within it, we can train and prepare ourselves to do so at the end of this incarnation while making our experience on Earth as pleasant as possible.

Those who have done a significant amount of inner work to release the energetic weight of their traumas, those who have overcome knee-jerk reactions to triggers, those who have mastered their minds and emotions, and those who are engaged in daily spiritual practices that allow them to regulate their nervous systems and find inner balance within their mind-body-spirit construct, will find themselves living in a reality that resonates with their achieved higher frequency and closely resembles the "promised land" of 5D.

Their lives will be lighter and easier than those of their neighbors. Their relationships will be more peaceful, and the manifestation of their desires into fulfillment will be faster and easier too. This is true.

The degree and consistency to which we are able to experience ourselves in the 5D state within Earth's reality depends on our specific energetic frequency and mainly on our ability to sustain it continuously.

Many flicker in and out of 4D and 5D, while sustaining the frequency resonance required to remain in 5D for good is generally challenging.

Doing the deep inner healing work is essential if we want to get anywhere near the 5D state; plus, it helps us become less of a target for the Archons as our daily loosh production lessens significantly or, if successful, potentially stops altogether. And then you are in 5D while still alive!

For an average human being, the above is hardly an achievable task, and thus, we keep longing for a better experience on Earth while trying to get ourselves there, suffering about it, and being a valuable "loosh factory" for the Archons.

As long as we want, hope for, or chase after something, we are producing the energy of loosh that feeds the Matrix. The deeper our dissatisfaction with our everyday life, the more loosh we produce, and the handlers of the reincarnation cycle are all over this human condition.

The afterlife promises to fulfill our earthly desires in the next incarnation is a tactic widely employed by the Archons. The stronger you hopelessly desire something in this lifetime, the more motivated you will be to return and have it "fulfilled" in your next incarnation, or so you are promised by the handlers.

This is literally the strongest motivation for average human subjects to keep returning and repeating physical life cycles again and again.

Do these promises ever get fulfilled? It certainly doesn't appear so. Plus, why would the system give away something that helps it collect the very energy that sustains it?

Let's take the example of someone who lost their loved one in this life, be that through death or a breakup, and the longing to be with that person lingers for the rest of one's life.

To lure you into your next incarnation, the handlers might promise that you will spend your entire next life together with that very soul. Few will not accept this offer with great joy.

Yet, in your next life, you might find that the soul you longed to be in a relationship with is now your mother or child. Spending your entire life in a relationship with them will indeed be true, but is it what you hoped for? Not even close.

PART THREE
5D and Dimensional Structure

As above, so below.

This stands for many things, and most definitely for the Matrix system, which continues to operate within the afterlife dimension and the astral plane around Earth.

I posit that the part of the astral dimension that we know as 5D is within the upper astral realm.

It is calm, peaceful, and beautiful, yet the passed-on subjects taking a rest there between incarnations maintain the entanglement with their earthly connections, experiences, and desires.

The "wiping" of most of these memories comes right before we enter the next cycle of physicality.

As I started to really question the fifth dimension throughout the year that followed my writing of "LEAVING THE TRAP," I received many downloads that helped me clarify the uncomfortable feeling I had about 5D beliefs.

I questioned why my system was intuitively responding with a "cat out of a bathtub" reaction when the fifth-dimensional extraterrestrials tried to channel through me in private sessions.

I remembered that the one time when I allowed that to happen, the channeling felt heavy and out of alignment with the familiar higher consciousness state.

The picture was painting itself, but given how much great stuff we are conditioned to believe about 5D, I wanted to make sure for myself. In one of my deep meditations, I decided to examine the fifth dimension more closely.

I wanted to know if 5D was still a part of the Matrix and the reincarnation cycle or if the worlds, planets, and beings operating on the level of 5D consciousness were trapped within the Matrix and the reincarnation system.

I received a visual of smaller bubbles that represented individual worlds and realities of various dimensions, places, planets, galaxies, and universes, all encapsulated under the electric-like border grid.

The visual included somewhat blurred images of various beings, their actions, and levels of consciousness. It resembled a diagram with dimensional "borders" vaguely marked as they flickered in and out of each other.

The "diagram" started with 2D, as the representation of the plant and animal kingdom, elemental spirits, and the non-physical spirit life operating on the second-dimensional level of consciousness.

Then came 3D-3.5D, representing the physical human realm and the lower consciousness spirits, including the disincarnate human souls attached to the physical hosts.

4D was the next layer, not significantly different from 3.5D, yet a bit lighter, both in expressions within physicality and in the consciousness of its non-physical life.

The realm or the level of consciousness around 4.5D was mostly shown as the human "dream reality," the dimension where we and many non-physical life forms dwell during unconscious sleep. It still had all of the emotional discomforts of the human reality and also non-human presence.

4.5D to 5D was the lighter consciousness space with a wide variety of spirits as well as human lucid dreaming, astral projecting, and various levels of deep meditative states. Perhaps we could call this layer "a mid-astral" plane.

5D was shown as one of the lighter layers of the Earth's Matrix system and a part of the reincarnation cycle.

In the non-physical, 5D was a part of the upper-astral plane, which we are taught to refer to as "the Heavenly Realm," the lightest and the highest in consciousness, compared to that of the previous dimensions: beautiful, peaceful, and comfortable.

This was also where the Archons flickered in and out of sight, disappearing and re-appearing as apparitions in various forms, including that of the Heavenly angelic-looking beings.

The energetic flow from the rest of the dimensions into 5D was represented by light-colored streams of energy, sound, and color and appeared to fuel the Archonic reality, guaranteeing its vitality. In a weird way, these streams resembled thick clusters of transparent fiber-optic cables.

Unsurprisingly, when the New Age beliefs tell us about living in 5D, it is referred to as "Heaven on Earth."

The sixth dimension appeared to be like fuzzy grey static, conscious yet shapeless and formless. As I tried to create a metaphor for the visual, I realized it resembled what some of us remember seeing on screens of old-school black-and-white TVs when the programs were over.

6D was where my vision of dimensional structure ended that night, and I had not re-addressed the rest of the dimensions as the answer about 5D that I was seeking was received.

Since this vision occurred, I quite unexpectedly had a conversation with someone who was helping to transition souls out of the cycle of reincarnation. This person mentioned that bringing and dropping off disincarnate souls who desired the way out of the reincarnation cycle past the fifth and sixth dimensions was imperative.

In Chapter 43 of the "Autobiography of a Yogi" by Paramahansa Yogananda, his Guru, Sri Yukteswar, describes the reality within the astral plane where his soul transitioned after passing.

The planet Sri Yukteswar was now on wasn't Earth but was within the astral realm.

It appeared to be considerably lighter and more pleasant than Earth, but it still had "astral Karma," and the inhabitants were still putting great effort into "clearing that Karma" in order to be liberated completely.

They also either rested on that planet after Earth incarnations or cross-incarnated between the reality of that planet and Earth plane under the pretext of paying off even more Earth Karma.

The way Sri Yukteswar described the planet and the reality of that planet was quite identical to what we know as 5D.

I highly recommend that you read this chapter of the "Autobiography of a Yogi" by Paramahansa Yogananda, as, quite unintentionally, it sheds light on the astral realm and the entrapment layers of the reincarnation cycle.

I contemplated the dimensional position of other planets that my friend Lee, whose near-death experience I described in "LEAVING THE TRAP," was offered to go to by the handlers instead of returning to Earth.

You might recall that he was shown some other planets where life was easier and lighter, yet he knew that these planets were still within the dimensional structure of the reincarnation cycle.

As above, so below, and thus it appears that we have the astral reality mirroring the Earth Matrix reality to a T. The astral realm encompasses the realities of other planets and undoubtedly includes what we know as the fifth dimension.

In the revolutionary British documentary "The Great Unknown," dedicated solely to the subject of death and the afterlife, Darius J. Wright says that there are twelve dimensions within the Matrix and the afterlife construct. I heard other sources mention fifteen.

Whatever the actual number might be, if there is even a way to count, the idea confirms that the fifth dimension is right in the middle of the Matrix and the reincarnation structure.

CHAPTER TWO
ETs. The Archons and the Angels

PART ONE
ETs

I was curious to know if other planets and other cosmic races had the same Matrix and reincarnation system as Earth and how it worked for them.

In my visions, I saw the "bubbles" of different worlds under the umbrella of the multi-galactic reincarnation system.

The Matrix system and the reincarnation cycle structure were universal and stretched across many dimensional levels.

The only difference between Earth's reincarnation cycle and that of other planets was in the way the beings that ran and benefited from the system, the handlers or the Archons, appeared to their subjects.

They no longer looked like Heavenly angelic beings but like the members of the cosmic races they were presenting themselves to.

This makes perfect sense, as popping in while looking like a humanoid Angel would be rather strange to a non-humanoid cosmic race.

Do these worlds have similar systems of belief as ours, the systems that make them prostrate before the apparitions of the glowing figures the way we do before Angelic-looking ones? What are the tactics used by the handlers in their worlds? Are their handlers the same as ours but present themselves in a way that's appropriate for their realities? Or is it all one big system projected differently into different worlds?

Good questions.

An even better question is this: who are the Archons hiding behind the shape-shifting fake facades? What type of beings are they? And are they beings at all or simply a holographic projection generated by advanced non-terrestrial technology?

At the present time, all we can do is speculate together, as no one really knows for sure quite yet.

I'd like to offer you a few concepts to probe deeper, research, and explore.

In her 2018 public interview with Lucas Alexander of "The Age of Truth TV," Linda Moulton Howe, a renowned American investigative journalist and Emmy award-winning documentary filmmaker mentioned her conversation with a Defense Intelligence official.

This official allegedly told her that the United States Government had proof of three competing geopolitical territorial intelligences using, mining, harvesting, and interacting on our planet and in this Solar System for at least 270 million years.

Hearing this made me jump out of my seat: are the three types of beings I saw at people's death beds (little blue beings, the Mantian-looking insectoid beings, and the Angelic-looking ones) representing the three intelligences that Linda spoke about? And if they are, which cosmic races are they, and which areas of space are they from?

The insectoid Mantians appear to be quite obvious. The "little blue beings" resemble the typical depictions of the "Greys" to such a degree that they could be the avatars for just about any cosmic race. Same as the Greys, they could also be consciousness-bearing biological technology.

But what about the Angelic-looking ones? Are they the "Nordic" Pleiadians they so strongly resemble?

According to many alternative sources, the "Nordic" Pleiadians have been interacting with humanity from the very inception of the human race, working with and infiltrating our governments and Earth population, setting bases and colonies on our planet, and influencing the course of history all along.

Are these the same beings as the Angelic-looking ones? Or can the Nordics be an entirely different cosmic race altogether?

In his brilliant book "Escaping from Eden: Does Genesis Teach that the Human Race was Created by God or Engineered by ETs?", Paul Wallis, a researcher, speaker, and author on spirituality and mysticism, who worked as a theological educator and an Archdeacon for the Anglican Church in Australia, and whose extensive work I highly recommend; brings to our attention the book of Genesis and other Biblical texts and their interpretations, that not only mention the beings humanity was conditioned to view as their "Gods," but also as their "Angels."

Paul Wallis posits that if we read these texts closely and translate them correctly, it appears that the "Angels" were not only "the messengers" of these "Gods" to humanity but the same exact type of being as the "Gods" themselves!

This puts all the beings that humanity was trained to worship and obey without question into the same category.

Were these beings part of the army of the Anunnaki, Pleiadians, or Archons, who installed their systems on Earth, including the reincarnation cycle? Were they the ones who created and used humanity for their needs while having the humans worship them as Gods? And were they the ones who ran and are still running our planet?

Lots to ponder here, no doubt.

PART TWO
The Angels and the Archons

What about all of the good things that the Angels are known for, like saving people's lives, helping them heal, and giving them helpful guidance? How could they be the Archons? And if they are, can the Angels thus be trusted?

I received the answer in one of the recent private sessions.

It is indeed true that the Angels will show up and help the humans, but the relationship between the humans and the Angels mirrors that between the humans and their farm and lab animals.

These animals are fed, protected, and cared for by humans, but only until it's "dinner time" or until it's time to use them for scientific experiments. In other words, there is an agenda behind keeping the human stock alive on Earth, not exactly happy but alive and getting by okay, in order for them to keep producing loosh.

Is the help to the humans real? Yes, it is. Real lives are saved, and real "miracles" are created for their human subjects. This elicits trust, devotion, and dedication to follow the instructions of the

Angels without question, and they might pop in again and give such instructions in the future.

Miraculous stories of help "from above" are shared by those who had these experiences, which entices their listeners to develop the same kinds of trusting beliefs. And thus, we are looking at a part of a very clever marketing campaign.

This brings up the question that is becoming more and more common within the spiritual community. Who are the trustworthy Spirit Guides if the Angels serve the Matrix and the reincarnation system?

I shall once again refer to the same private session where the download about the Angels was received. Here is what I got.

If the Spirit Guides pop in and start giving guidance without an invitation, watch out for an agenda. The information given might be totally valid and assist the person receiving it while on Earth, but eventually, the agenda will reveal itself through requests to perform this or that function in the name of the "higher good" or without any explanation whatsoever.

The extreme inadequacy of the human condition made the people who the Angels told that they were "the chosen ones" experience a sense of importance they had never known. They felt a sense of higher purpose and the notion that their existence actually mattered and could serve what they believed was the higher good.

Have you ever wondered why so many of the "chosen ones" were simple, uneducated, and highly religious people who were not about to question the motives of the beings in front of them or the outcomes of what was requested of them? These people simply prostrated before the beings in utter devotion and went on to fulfill what they were told without question.

This continues to the present day, not that the subjects who suddenly start receiving guidance to go here and there or do this and that are uneducated, but that they still follow what they are told without question. The underlying belief that whatever the beings are telling them is for the highest good is still there to this day. But is it true?

Let's take the example of Joan of Arc, who was a real historical figure. Joan was a young girl who, at the age of thirteen, experienced a vision of Archangel Michael accompanied by two Saints appearing before her in a beam of blasting white light. These Divine-looking beings told her that her mission was to save France by putting a certain figure in power.

Simple, religious, and uneducated, Joan was strongly impacted by the appearance of the glowing figures before her and was easily convinced that she was "the Chosen One" to carry out the mission of "God's Will." She had full conviction that the words of Archangel Michael were a direct message from God.

Once her dedication to follow what she was told without questioning was established through the initial meeting, the guidance continued to be delivered to her telepathically.

Although she was still very young and in doubt of her own abilities to lead the armies, Joan was instructed to gather the troops and embark on the mission she was guided to fulfill. With "God's Help," she was successful until the task was accomplished.

The immense loss of life that the whole endeavor resulted in tormented her pure heart but didn't seem to concern the otherworldly beings in the slightest. She wept on the fields of massacre left behind her throughout her campaign but pressed on in the name of "God's Will."

Joan completed the task of putting a certain figure on the throne and a certain family in power. This changed the power dynamic between England and France.

If we analyze the outcome of the situation from the present-day perspective, it becomes quite obvious that the driving objective behind the whole endeavor was to influence the power dynamic between these countries.

It was nothing more than mere politics that had little to do with "God's Will," something we find the Archons and the servers of the Matrix system involved in to this day.

What happened to Joan once the objective was fulfilled? Where did the "Divine Messengers" and the "God's Help" go when she was tortured, imprisoned, and sold to the enemy, declared a heretic, and burnt at the stake at the tender age of nineteen? Did the "Messengers of God" step up to save her or to ease her destiny? We all know they didn't.

Joan was no longer of any use for the Archonic agenda, so, as it happens to this very day, she was abandoned and discarded, while the glowing Divine-looking beings had no mercy and no compassion for her.

PART THREE
AI & Holographic Simulation Theory

Artificially generated holographic simulation reality theory is in circulation nowadays, so another question presents itself, and I encourage you to look into it.

What is all that "grey static" within the sixth dimension? Why do the Archons only appear in visible form in some dimensions of the Matrix and not in others?

How many people die on Earth every day, and how many Archons are needed to greet them in the afterlife?

Could the handlers we experience in the afterlife simply be holographic simulations generated by highly advanced extraterrestrial artificial intelligence technology that can scan our consciousness and produce images in accordance with what we believe in?

Could the sixth dimension, or any of the 12-15 dimensions others have mentioned, be the layer where that technology was eventually set up to generate the above-mentioned holographic simulation, in order to free the Archonic life-forms from having to deal with the humans one-on-one; while simultaneously maintaining the benefits of collecting loosh for their energetic sustenance?

Considering how many variations of the afterlife dimension we hear about from those who had NDEs or just explored these realms through astral projecting, the idea of a simulation that simply scans our minds and generates the visual environments that our beliefs resonate with the most, is quite plausible.

There is also the fact that a false presentation of just about every natural occurrence exists within dimensions of the Matrix. There is a simulation of the cosmos, a simulation of the True Light, and even a simulation of the True Void. (Read more on this and on how to tell the difference in the final chapter of this book.)

I'm sure that the answers to the puzzle are to be revealed in due time.

And in the meantime, I invite you to research, ponder, or meditate on these possibilities, if only to entertain your inquisitive minds while simultaneously engaging in the advanced spiritual practices that prepare you for the quantum jump out of dimensions of the

Matrix, the reincarnation system, and the simulation altogether.

CHAPTER THREE
Samadhi, Kundalini and the True Void

PART ONE
Kundalini Awakening, 2014

What is possible when we use the "spiritual technology" of the Cosmic Cobra Breath and nighttime meditation, and what are the indications that we are on the right track? Allow me to share more of my own experiences just to demonstrate how the journey deepens if we don't give up, and how exciting it could be.

Around 3:30 AM Monday morning, during a super-intense thunderstorm, I sat up to meditate. I did the Cosmic Cobra Breath, cleared my mind, pulled the energy out of the lower centers to activate the upper, opened my heart, and was probably sitting for about an hour, seeing nothing but colors, bright dots, and geometric shapes floating in darkness.

The meditation seemed pretty "uneventful," and I felt my body wanting to lie down. I was taught to stay seated past this point, and although I was a bit bored, I kept sitting up cross-legged with my spine straight and my back against the wall.

All of a sudden, quite "out of the blue," I started experiencing waves of goosebumps running up my spine, coupled with heat and an immense emotion of love, a sensation so strong that it almost immediately moved me to tears. My breathing intensified, my heartbeat became loud and rapid, and the waves of heat and goosebumps became stronger and stronger.

I could feel sweat rolling down my body, then the body started shaking uncontrollably, and then I felt as if the back and the top of my head blew open, and a wild river of energy moved up through my entire physical form and out of the top of my head.

I became absorbed in internally observing the phenomenon of my body turning into a cloud of glowing particles held together by intense energy.

First, my arms and hands felt like blazing beams of light, and then the rest of my physical form turned into a blinding column of light and disappeared in a flash. The visual was similar to my body exploding into light. I was later told that I was screaming, but I didn't hear any of it.

Everything went still after the "explosion," and I was gone.

The transition was instant. I found myself floating in the vast dark nothingness, the ocean of blackness without space and time, so far away from my physical body that it felt like I couldn't move a finger if my life depended on it. Not like I had a finger to move at that point.

It felt so good, so familiar; I wanted to remain in this state forever! I existed, and at the same time, the "I" that I knew didn't exist. "Normal" human emotions were no longer with me: I felt no fear, no anger, no sadness, no worry, no pain, and no hurt of any sort.

Instead, I felt *a tremendous amount of LOVE*. I didn't know this kind of love was possible. I felt complete oneness with everything, complete peace, and the certainty that everything in my life so far made perfect sense.

Tears of absolute bliss were rolling down my face somewhere far, far away, but I had no awareness of it... I had no idea how much time went by on Earth while I was in this unforgettable state.

Then there was a shift and something else started happening. Emerging out of the dark space one by one were the eyes of the people I knew in this life. I saw every person I've ever loved, every client I've ever worked with, every one of my friends, my parents, my family, both living and passed on—hundreds of people whom I sensed individually and also as a collective all at once, everyone from my entire extended Soul Group.

Great sorrow came over me as I could feel as my own the incredible sadness of the human experience of these brilliant souls on Earth, lost in their daily struggles and strives, pain, suffering, desires, and aspirations…

I felt love and compassion towards them of a magnitude I never consciously experienced before. This was the moment when I understood what the concept of "Christ Consciousness" that is talked about so much in metaphysical circles nowadays really means and what Jesus, Krishna, Buddha, Gurus, Saints, and true Spiritual Masters felt for humanity.

This understanding was so profound it had a tremendous impact on my life.

More "no time" passed, and eventually, I was able to lay my body down, after which I found myself in a state of "sleep paralysis." I was unable to "operate" my physical form; I couldn't turn my head or move my limbs.

At the same time, my consciousness was completely awake, and suddenly my awareness was filled with every detail of the room. Lying on my back face up, with my eyes closed and the eye mask on, I could still see and also smell every object in my room.

In parallel with this intensified awareness of the details of the room, I was simultaneously experiencing myself as other people and other beings living other lives in other places and times. It was both fascinating and unbelievable, as all of it was happening at the same time! I had no idea my brain had the capacity to process and observe so many things at once.

It felt like thousands of years and many incarnations went by, but the entire meditation was only a couple of hours long. Forever changed, I was back in my body when the alarm went off, and it was time to get up and start my day.

I just described my first experience of Kundalini awakening and the third-eye activation due to the Cosmic Cobra Breath and the nighttime meditation technique I was practicing for less than a year at that point.

As I continued to practice, I had innumerable fascinating experiences since.

I am not alone in this, as people who engage in similar practices without giving up reach the point when they start having profound experiences, and everything I describe in this chapter becomes available to them.

Maintaining this practice nightly for ten years (2014-2024) has been most rewarding for me.

If, like me, you like to experiment, you can teach yourself to utilize this practice in various different ways.

I never teach what I haven't experienced myself, so below are a few things for you to look forward to that I can attest to firsthand.

We can connect the practice of the Cosmic Cobra Breath coupled with the nighttime meditation with the ability to hop out of the reincarnation cycle by learning how to navigate our non-physical form while still alive.

We can learn to use the same practice to clear our subconscious minds during the inner healing work, which is a prerequisite to getting out of the reincarnation cycle.

We can teach ourselves to use our Kundalini energy to go out of body at will and quantum travel back to The Void and the Infinite Field of Source and to fascinating higher realities too.

When you feel so inclined to have your quantum travel adventures, you can use the practice to view and experience parallel timelines and your soul's inter-dimensional other lives.

We can learn to facilitate deliberate timeline jumps, getting ourselves out of situations that we do not prefer and, if we are really good at it, instantly shift out of physical ailments. I have to admit this one is still a hit or miss for me, although I've had enough "hits" to know that this is possible!

Cosmic Cobra Breath and nighttime meditations help us continuously improve our lives and expand our "paranormal" abilities.

Doing this practice brings us to know who we really are as infinite souls. It offers the awareness of our True Omnipresent Self while in the human body on Earth, and thus, it paves the way to *the ultimate soul freedom*.

I know nothing more rewarding than the practice of the Cosmic Cobra Breath and the nighttime meditation.

PART TWO
Deliberate Timeline Jumping

When we become really good at navigating the non-physical, deliberate timeline jumps could be facilitated with the use of the Cosmic Cobra breath and meditation. We are still doing it within the Matrix system, but it helps to make our Earth plane lives better.

By no means have I mastered this, but I have had a few timeline jumps that were so obvious that they left no shadow of a doubt in my mind as to how they were facilitated. But before I give you a real example, let's look at the phenomenon of timeline jumping as a whole.

Timeline jumps happen all the time; they are a part of our daily, even hourly, reality, happening countless times per second, but the outcomes of this process are too minute for most of us to notice.

Those with strong observation skills and who know what to look for might notice minor details of reality being different from the day before or from what they might remember.

For example, remembering that a plant outside of your home was on the left side of the door or window and then suddenly noticing that it was now on the right.

Or knowing for sure that an electronic device had been broken for a while and then finding it working perfectly fine without having been looked at or repaired.

When the symptoms of a timeline shift are as obvious as these, a person noticing them usually feels "different" about themselves too, while often not being able to quite explain the way in which they are different exactly.

Here is an example of a timeline jump that I experienced and facilitated through daytime meditation and the Cosmic Cobra Breath technique.

A few years back, an accountant I used told me that I had to pay $5,000 in taxes during the tax season. It was a desperate time for me, and paying $5,000 was simply not possible.

Not knowing what to do and how to get out of this situation, I decided to do the Cosmic Cobra Breath and sit in meditation with the intention of pulling myself away from this whole story. I was sure that, if anything, I was going to feel much better afterward.

I had no idea if I could change anything or how, but my intent was very strong. I remember repeating to myself, "This is not my story," while pulling myself out of my body with the breath-work.

The meditation turned out to be quite deep, and when it was over, my whole tax payment dilemma seemed like a distant dream.

I looked at my phone, and there was a message from a friend.

She wrote: "I was just thinking of you and wondering if you could use any tax help this year; I am an accountant and would be happy to do the taxes for you."

To begin with, I didn't know that this friend did taxes, plus my usual accountant was in New York, and I was already in Arizona, so I gladly accepted her offer.

After my friend went through my paperwork, she happily informed me that the government would pay me $5,000 that year in tax return money.

Needless to say, my jaw was on the floor, and the flip of the story from one to the polar opposite was indeed the biggest deliberate timeline jump I had experienced so far.

Going forward with the practice, I started noticing more and more frequently that when I came back into the body after the meditation and especially after the quantum travel experiences, all I could see in my room when I opened my eyes was a blinding golden light.

It appeared that it took physical reality a bit of time to form itself around me again, and more often than not, I found peculiar little differences between how things were then compared to the day before.

This included physical changes like having a spot on my leg before meditation and not having it after, being able to stop the flu from developing if I meditated at the very start of it, or just feeling like I left one body and returned to a different one.

I know this might sound far-fetched to those who have never experienced things like this, but those who have would certainly know firsthand what I am talking about.

PART THREE
Birthday Meditation and Sri Yukteswar

Publishing "LEAVING THE TRAP" led to many unexpected conversations and eye-opening new discoveries. One of these powerful conversations was my interview with Trey Downes of "Your Superior Self."

Trey asked me three questions that led to a mystical experience, incredible realizations, and a new level of awareness.

He asked if the practice I did mid-sleep was a part of Kriya Yoga, if I knew who Babaji was, and if I had any non-physical interactions with the Yogic Ascended Masters. My answer to all three was a "no," but my curiosity was piqued, so I began a little research.

The first thing I found out was that the breathwork (Cosmic Cobra Breath) and the meditative practice (mid-sleep meditations) I've been doing nightly for the last ten years were indeed a part of Kriya yoga, "Babaji's greatest gift to humanity."

According to Paramahansa Yogananda's description in his "Autobiography of a Yogi,"

Kriya Yoga is a yogic technique that helps still sensory turmoil and allows a person to achieve an ever-increasing communion with cosmic consciousness.

This, I felt, explained why my priorities in life changed so much once I started doing the practice.

Then, shortly thereafter, a miraculous occurrence took place during my birthday meditation and also the night before that.

My birthday meditations are extra-long, and I do them during the morning hours on the day of my birth (not mid-sleep). But the night before my birthday, Sri Yukteswar Giri, Paramahansa Yogananda's Guru, came into my dream.

His face appeared in my dream, and looked at me intensely in silence. This woke me up as if someone was in my room, and I was very surprised. The dream appearance was so strong that it took me a while to get back to sleep.

The next morning, I got up and started my birthday meditation. I had questions and also wanted to dive in deep on my special day. What happened next was beyond my wildest expectations.

As soon as my "monkey mind" let go and I entered a deep meditative state, Sri Yukteswar Giri appeared again. He simply stepped into the periphery of my inner vision and positioned himself on its right in a way that allowed me to still have the visuals I was having, while his glowing silhouette and the unmistakably recognizable face were visible to me too.

After about an hour, Sri Yukteswar was still there, doing nothing else except calmly observing me, so I addressed this presence with a question. I simply asked, with my deepest respect, if he was going to just sit there and watch me the entire time. The answer I got was a simple nod.

I started telling him that I was not to be convinced to do anything, that I knew my path and was not available to be directed one way or another. I wanted to set this boundary right away, as I wanted him to know that I was not interested in a Guru, be that in the physical or the non-physical form.

Additionally, given that the apparition showed up without an invitation, I wasn't sure if he was the real Sri Yukteswar Giri or if an Archon was posing as him. This suspicion eventually eased as I realized that no unsolicited guidance was given and that the apparition of Sri Yukteswar was only there to observe me.

He calmly watched me while I delivered all of the above, gave no response, and didn't move, just continued looking at me. His presence remained poised and calm, the same as when he first appeared.

One of the questions I intended to pose during my birthday meditation was the time and the way of my final departure from Earth at the end of this life.

My biggest aspiration for my personal development during what's left of this lifetime is to reach such a level of mastery over matter and energy as to be able to facilitate the circumstances and the time of my bodily death, the same as many yogic masters, including Paramahansa Yogananda and Sri Yukteswar Giri did.

At the end of this birthday meditation, right as the glowing silhouette of Sri Yukteswar Giri started to fade out of my inner vision, I received an instant download of the time and the circumstance of my death, the precise way my present physical life on Earth will be complete.

PART FOUR
The First High Samadhi

I woke up to 53 degrees in the house, later than my usual meditation time; it was almost 5 am. My mind tried to talk me into staying in a warm bed and skipping the meditation, yet a part of me was excited to get up and do the practice.

After I did the breathwork and sat for a while working on my field and processing the imprints of my previous day, I noticed a feeling of increasing inner silence pulling me deeper into itself. I felt my heart chakra activating, vibrating, swelling, and heating up.

There was a flush of light, and everything shifted. Suddenly, the room was filled with the smell of heavenly flowers, a scent I could not place as nothing in my house smelled this way.

The temperature in the room appeared to turn perfect, as if on a perfect summer day; suddenly my body was no longer cold.

As the indescribable bliss started to engulf me, pulling me further and farther away from the awareness of the body, I noticed my heartbeat slowing down more and more until it ceased completely, and so did my breathing. Everything in my body became utterly still.

These observations were the last faint thoughts of the mind before it went the most silent it had ever been. My awareness of myself and my body disappeared and I dissolved into the field of infinity.

The rest is hard to put into words. The state of Divine Cosmic Omnipresence is what I became; the black ocean of the Absolute that encompassed everything and nothing.

Strangely enough, the experience of the "heavenly scent" was still there, although I had no nostrils to receive it. I was in the state of indescribable bliss; the state of unity with Infinite Source; the stillness, the peace, and the consciousness of everything… It was absolutely divine and I wanted to remain this way forever!

I have experienced Samadhi countless times, but this was different. I've never gone this deep before. I've never had the body stop breathing (normally very slow and shallow breath still remained). I've never experienced cessation of heartbeat, the "heavenly scent" and the change in room temperature. I've never attained this level of silence of the mind.

I normally find myself back in the body "automatically" once the meditative music is over. This time I had to make a decision to return and "restart" my functions while my entire essence resisted.

My mind returned first, calling me, saying that it was time to go back. Like an outside observer, I heard it and made an effort to pull myself back into the body. My entire essence protested, as all I wanted was to remain the way I was, in the indescribable bliss, away from physical life.

The "heavenly scent" vanished; the perfect temperature vanished too, I felt cold again. I entered the body, took a few deliberately deep breaths, and my heartbeat restarted. I made my body move its arms and legs, just to see that I still could. It felt heavy as lead.

Without a shadow of a doubt, I now knew that the force animating my flesh and keeping it alive was me.

And there I was, back in the physical, but forever changed.

I later learned from Yogananda's writings that what I experienced was the breathless and motionless trance of Sabikalpa Samadhi, in which Christian, Muslim, Hindu, and non-Hindu mystics have been observed while in the first stages of God-perception.

I suspect that most of these mystics managed to find their way out of the trap, and for obvious reasons we would never know the details of their escape.

PART FIVE
Practicing the "Mini-Death"

I remember being a part of the primordial field, way before form, thought, or consciousness. It is the state that cannot be put into words, the feeling of Home beyond any description. The mere memory of it brings tears to my eyes.

"Die before you die," the Sufi mystics teach us, and following this recommendation is the main part of successfully training yourself to exit the cycle of rebirth.

This concept isn't to be mistaken with stopping to live within your current life. This idea has never referred to bringing all of your human activities to a halt, isolating, and becoming frozen in life in any way, shape, or form.

What the Sufis refer to is getting comfortable with the practice of experiencing the "mini-death" while still alive, and by "mini-death," they mean the state of higher awareness beyond the body, the state we call Samadhi.

Training yourself to have deliberate out-of-body experiences and the experiences of various levels of Samadhi, especially the high Samadhi, such as Sabikalpa that I had described earlier, is indeed exactly that: the practice of your "mini-death."

When you engage in The Cosmic Cobra Breath and the nighttime meditation on a daily basis, you start having experiences that allow you to differentiate between your physical and non-physical self, and thus, the perishing of the body is no longer perceived as something terrifying.

You lose the fear of death and gain the ability to control your life-force, direct your non-physical form in and out of the body, and free yourself from the shackles of physicality that the Matrix and rebirth systems are wired into, once and for all.

And the longer you practice, the easier it becomes until you find slipping in and out of your body and quantum hopping out of the earth-bound systems to be quite effortless. This I can tell you with full certainty.

Some of you might find yourselves there pretty fast, but most will need to overcome the egoic question, "are we there yet?" and have both discipline and patience. You are not living in a monastery where you could meditate for twelve hours a day, and within our dense and hectic lifestyles, getting there takes time.

Only gradually, after ten years of practicing the Cosmic Cobra Breath and the nighttime meditations, did I arrive at the point where the experience of returning home to the primordial field became quite seamless. It is no longer drastic in any way.

My body no longer burns, screams, or shakes, and most of the time, the transition out of physicality is quiet and easy.

I've also been noticing that even the breath-work isn't always required anymore, but only because, throughout the years of deliberation, I've already blazed my trail out, made it familiar, and am simply following it now.

Going home into the Absolute is an experience blissful beyond words, yet at times, I still weep right before I completely dissolve and lose all sense of my humanness.

I weep from my soul's recognition of its home and the awareness of how I long to return to being just that, from how remote and separate the limited human experience is from our true infinite essence, and also from this indescribable feeling that comes over me right before I lose touch with all human emotion; the feeling of the deepest soul-level remembrance.

All death really is the separation from the physical body, and so you can say that I have been practicing my "mini-death" for years. I believe I know exactly how my physical death is going to go, as I feel I have developed the skill to make my final departure exactly the way I prefer it to be.

After experiencing the indescribable state of the Absolute so many times, I think that shedding the restraints of the physical body is liberation for me.

And at the end of this cycle on Earth, when my human physicality finally stops tugging on me once and for all, I look forward to dissolving back into our Primordial Home, never to be forced to come back here again.

CHAPTER FOUR
Death is Not the End

PART ONE
My Dead Father and I

I dedicate this Chapter to my late Father, who was a scientifically-minded atheist and didn't believe in spirit life, not till after he passed anyway.

It was the summer of 2022, and weird man-made illnesses were going around. In the middle of the otherwise uneventful night of July 28, I woke up from a sudden urge to vomit.

Three days later, I was still dry heaving but was now unable to get myself up from my bed. The jar of water next to me was empty, but making an effort to get more was useless: the body was violently rejecting even the tiniest drop.

I simply lay there while the functions of my body shut down one by one. I was no longer able to get up, urinate, eat, or drink water; breathing was becoming more and more difficult; the entire body was in agonizing pain. Only my heart seemed to still have life in it, pounding and fluttering in my chest harder and faster than I'd ever known possible.

My phone was next to me, but I didn't think to grab a charger when I got it from the kitchen in the middle of the first night of this unsolicited adventure. There was as little battery life in it now as in my own physical body.

The last thing my phone did before shutting itself down was deliver a voicemail message that seemed to occur out of nowhere. Although I had no energy to talk, I had a strong feeling to listen to the voicemail.

It was my mother's voice with somber words all the way from across the world: "Your father died this morning." It was July 31st.

I closed my eyes as my phone went dead in my hand. I felt so ill and exhausted I couldn't even cry.

Left behind by his mother when his father was taken into the concentration camp during WWII, my father was raised in an orphanage. Although his life was full of extreme hardship, disappointment, and betrayal, he still maintained faith in humanity and had kindness, honor, and integrity. He selflessly served the bigger picture, always available to everyone in need, leaving little time for his own family.

Given how little we interacted since I moved away, with parents living in a different country and father having no predisposition towards lengthy catch-up calls, I always teased him that we were going to spend way more time together after his death.

He wasn't a believer in any such thing and always laughed as if it was the biggest joke while firmly believing that his physical death was simply the end.

As he got older and frailer, and I was as stubborn in my own beliefs as he was in his, I insisted more and more often that I was going to find him after his passing.

And now that moment was here.

Given he had just let go of his body; I knew I had to go find him right away. I hoped to catch him and establish our connection before he was pulled too far away from the Earth plane.

I wasn't about to break my word regardless of how I felt, so I dropped into a really deep meditative state and embarked on the search for my father's soul. My body being ill wasn't much of an obstacle. Instead of my usual upright meditative position, I simply had to do the whole thing while allowing the body to keep lying down.

I kept calling out to Dad and found him within just a few moments.

All I was saying out into the empty space was: "Dad! Dad! Where are you? How are you doing out there?" As I got deeper into the Theta brain wave state, his voice suddenly came in, and I clearly heard him say: "It's good. I'm good. I just feel terrible for Mom."

I knew what he meant: they were married for over 50 years!

Although even in my altered state, I couldn't see him, I could hear his voice and was relieved that I found him.

I thought he must've still been within the Earth plane, but as much as I wanted to, I knew I couldn't hold him here. I knew he had to go on, and I had to go through a grieving process to release and forgive every little thing so that his soul could move on without the slightest trace of guilt.

It was mid-2022; I hadn't quite come to the level of expertise about the reincarnation cycle and the whole passing process that I have now. I didn't quite understand the need to release soul contracts to help both my and the other person's soul journey. But the intuitive knowing was there, and there was no better state to do the processing than lying flat in my bed.

I went all the way back to the vision I described in "LEAVING THE TRAP." The vision in which I remembered connecting with the spirits of my parents in a different reality, where we agreed that they were going to get together and facilitate my entry into this world.

It was a beautiful reality that felt like being inside a rainbow, the higher octave of the upper astral plane, as I now know.

My father wasn't one to back away from the reincarnation cycle or opt out of taking another incarnation. He didn't know about any of it and didn't believe in reincarnation, to begin with, so such an idea had never occurred to him. This meant he was going straight into the system, and it didn't feel like it was my place to interfere.

I simply wondered if he was about to find himself back within the same plane where our first soul meeting occurred.

Regardless of the great love and deep bond between us, our earthly relationship wasn't an easy one, so the grieving process was emotionally intense. Preoccupied with the idea that I needed to release Dad from all bonds and ties with me within the first week after his passing, I paid little attention to the condition of my own body, which kept progressing.

Headache, nausea, whole-body pain, pounding of the heart, difficulties breathing, indescribable exhaustion; all of it continued, but dry heaving stopped, and I was able to take in tiny sips of water.

Birds woke me up the next morning, and as I opened my eyes, I realized that I had gone blind. Interesting, I thought. My body is shutting down; perhaps it is my time to go too.

Now that I couldn't see, there wasn't a thing I could do about the body, but I was fully-conscious, so as I lay there with my eyes open into complete staticky darkness, I pushed on to finish the processing of our relationship with Dad.

Eventually, a moment of deep peace, forgiveness, and closure enveloped me, and for the first time since my father passed, I started crying.

Tears were choking me as I lay on my back, making it even more difficult to breathe. I rolled onto my stomach and got into a fetal position.

It was dark behind my sightless eyes. In complete blackness, I cried right into my already-soaked pillow. I was finally saying goodbye to my dad and to all that we had shared.

And then the light came. The experience was similar to when you might be in a pitch-black room with your eyes closed, and someone walks in with a bright flashlight and points it at your face. It appeared as if I could see the light through my closed eyelids.

This got my attention; I stopped crying, sat up, and opened my eyes. Blackness.

Oh, man, I thought, and I started crying even harder. Then, the blinding light appeared again. This time, I didn't open my eyes. I heard my father's voice clearly say: "I am right here, I didn't go anywhere, I am right here!"

I sat up and told him it was okay; he was free to go. I said I held nothing against him; I told him I was grateful for all that we had shared and that I loved him and wished him a peaceful journey.

And at that very moment, everything instantly changed.

I was no longer in my room. I was somewhere else, in a space of indescribable lightness, where I could no longer feel my body. I could see very clearly, and I was looking at my dad.

He looked like a transparent light figure. He was young, possibly around 30 years old. He was standing on a transparent rainbow road leading to a big Golden Gateway or Golden Portal. The portal was like a shimmering circle of golden light suspended in an open rainbow-colored space.

Dad was looking at me with great kindness and love, and without much conviction, as I was fairly certain my body wasn't dead yet, I said: "Dad, I'll come with you!" "No," he replied. "You cannot do that, but you can walk with me."

He turned around and started walking toward the shimmering Golden Portal. It didn't look like he was moving away, as if he was walking backward on a moving walkway. I took his arm, and side-by-side, we silently walked without moving an inch. Any amount of time could've passed. It was a strange experience as it was obvious that we weren't moving forward, yet we still walked to share these final moments together.

Then he freed himself from my arm, nodded, and stepped into the Golden Circle, and I was instantly back in my pain-ridden body that was lying face down in my bed.

I turned, opened my eyes, and saw the red digits of my clock in the naturally dark room. They looked blurry and illegible, but it wasn't pitch-black anymore. It was the night of August 3rd.

Of course, now that I've told this story, everyone is going to ask me if I was interacting with my father or with an Archon.

I'm pretty sure it was my father for two reasons. First, we met in the astral realm, the only place you can really meet with the spirit of a passed-on person, but we did not meet in the afterlife section of it. My dad was on the way to the afterlife section of the astral, but he wasn't there yet.

Second, he didn't want anything from me, didn't tell me to do or not to do anything. He also didn't send me back into my body but invited me to walk him to the "Pearly Gates," so to speak.

God only knows who or what met him for the life review on the other side of that golden entry.

PART TWO
Death is Not the End

After my father left this plane and went into the Golden Portal that led to the afterlife dimension, he started to regularly appear in my dreams, both with messages and without.

It was frequent and regular for about a year and a half after his passing. As a matter of fact, he was present as a bystander in almost all of my dreams, even the dreams where he did not belong at all.

In some of these dreams, he was simply sitting there, like an extra in a movie, and although I was dreaming, I was fully aware that he was visiting and was always glad that he stopped by and I got to see him.

He was definitely fulfilling my prediction of being there for me more than ever after his passing, but this didn't last. Towards the end of the second year, his visits became less and less frequent. I started thinking that he was getting ready to reincarnate again.

It is my current understanding of things that if after your passing you still want to be there for your loved ones, you have to go into the afterlife dimension.

This means you cannot opt for getting out of the cycle of rebirth. And eventually, after about three Earth years in the afterlife dimension, you will find yourself reincarnating back into the physical plane again.

My father was most definitely in the afterlife dimension. The Golden Portal was the entry point, and our walk through the astral plane preceded his entering the afterlife dimension.

It appears that he didn't go into the afterlife dimension immediately after his passing but spent about three days making his goodbyes after his physical body had died.

This is not uncommon, as many people report seeing their loved ones appear in their homes and in dreams immediately after their passing.

And then there are those who linger.

One of my clients told me about a friend who took his own life and then parked his spirit on that client's couch for quite some time, all due to the fear that hell awaited him.

When my neighbor and friend Patty passed away, I unmistakably sensed her presence both in her own home and in my house as well; and also at the place where she used to work.

Due to my gift of "psychic smelling," I could often psychically "smell" her standing right next to me in my own home and also at the store.

She worked at a neighborhood store and it wasn't uncommon that with my side vision I saw her walk by me in an aisle, but when I turned to look, no one was there.

It turned out later that I was not the only one who saw her at the store. To my great surprise, one of the cashiers told me that Patty was frequently seen around the store by the staff; and that when they called out her name and asked if she was there, she'd push things off the shelves in response.

I was also able to communicate with Patty, but her presence, the visions, the scent, and the ease of connecting with her gradually diminished towards the end of the second year after her passing.

There appears to be some flexibility to when the departed go into the afterlife dimension. Some seem to leave the Earth plane right away, some stick around for goodbyes, and others stay longer till they are ready.

And then, of course, there are the "ghosts" and the disincarnates who are the disembodied souls who attach either to places or to people and do not go into the afterlife dimension willingly, not until they are forced to anyway.

Although Patty seemed to have been around for much longer than I know as common, I am sure she eventually went into the afterlife dimension to take her next rebirth.

When she was alive, she often told me that she didn't do so well in this life and would have to come back and do better the next time around.

Such was her wish and her belief, and I have no doubt that this alone prompted her to go into the reincarnation cycle, if not right away, then eventually.

CHAPTER FIVE
Pets and Animals

PART ONE
Pets and Animals

What about animals and our beloved pets? Are they subject to being recycled within the reincarnation wheel too?

I'm afraid they are, and humans love it. There are movies about this, and we love sensing that our favorite dog, cat, or horse that we miss so much after their passing came back to us in a different body.

Humans form strong bonds with animals, and although animal lives are much shorter than those of humans, we can be quite sure that our furry companions will find their way back to us.

It appears that the animals we experience as pets are a part of the soul group we reincarnate with again and again. They never stray too far from their owners; some connections last over centuries of incarnations.

We hear many examples where people casually say, "I swear this cat used to be my dog; they do the same stuff!" or "I feel like I know this baby goat; it's almost like he is my passed-on horse; they are so alike!"

It appears that animals do not always reincarnate into the same type of bodies, although they often do. Dogs don't always come back as dogs, cats as cats, horses as horses, but they find their way into their beloved owner's lives nonetheless.

It also appears that souls that used to have animal bodies sometimes come back in human bodies too, and throughout my life, I have encountered more than one example of this.

I also remember myself being a lion and an eagle in my past incarnations, which I mentioned in "LEAVING THE TRAP."

I've encountered a number of people who appeared to be first human incarnations after being in animal bodies before.

One was a friend who, in his behavior, resembled a dog so much that I had a hard time perceiving him as a human. This was so odd for me that I actually convinced this friend to consult a psychic who did soul readings.

We didn't tell the psychic about this peculiarity that was haunting me; I just asked her to do a reading for my friend. Not without much astonishment, the psychic told us that when she went to do his past life reading, all she could see was a specific kind of dog.

The other encounter of the animal-to-human incarnation was so remarkable that I will dedicate a part of this chapter to telling you the story.

Through personal readings that I used to do where people asked about their pets, I have learned that it wasn't uncommon for cosmic souls to travel to Earth accompanied by their cosmic companions who took animal incarnations by their side, while others took on human forms.

In a number of sessions where I assisted animal spirits in their transition, I also found out that at least some of them, specifically the non-domesticated ones, were experiencing the same frustration about being stuck on Earth as awakened humans do, feeling limited and dumbed-down, unable to return to the planets of their origin.

PART TWO
Lana and Roxi

All I wanted my entire childhood was to have a dog. Not a day went by that I didn't pester my parents for one, and then finally, when the circumstances allowed and I was twelve years old, there she was! A tiny ball of black curly fur, my own sweet little puppy, my dream come true. I called her Lana.

Lana was a standard-size black poodle. I didn't want a poodle; I wanted a big, strong dog like a German shepherd or a Great Dane, but my parents got me a poodle, and that was it.

We formed a special connection from day one. It was my dog; I was in charge of everything about her. I fed, walked, and trained her, but I mainly shared a special secret bond with her, an understanding beyond words, a soul-to-soul connection.

Just an eye contact, a mere glance from me, was enough for her to know exactly what I was thinking and act accordingly.

I often observed her lying down in the same room as myself with her eyes open, following me with her gaze that was full of love and devotion so pure that it never failed to warm my troubled teenage heart.

There was something else that we did that was just ours. Lana didn't do the same thing with anyone else in the family: we hugged. I'd sit or kneel on the floor, and she'd come up to me, pressing her chest into mine, put her head on my shoulder, and just stand there while I held my hands around her neck.

These were the tender moments of calm closeness, and I could feel the heartbeat in her chest, as I knew she could feel mine. I cherished these hugs from the very start; there was something magical about them, and as I got older, they also helped me feel better at moments of sadness and distress.

For nine years, Lana was a part of my life. She was in good health, full of life and vigor, and wasn't showing any signs of aging. And then, the day came when I hugged her for the last time and moved across the world in search of a better life.

My parents wrote to me that Lana refused to leave my room after I left. She kept opening the door of the cabinet where my clothes were kept and spent her days with her head inside the cabinet, whimpering. She refused to eat and lost her ever-present enthusiasm for walks.

Then, in the same exact way as it happens with human beings, the constant pain of the broken heart formed a lump of matter in her chest, and shortly thereafter, Lana died of cancer.

According to the birth certificate of the well-bred racing Greyhound called Roxi, she entered this reality exactly on the day of my Lana's passing, except a few years later.

Eight years after that, I walked into the garden of the house I was thinking about renting in Sedona, AZ. The first thing I saw was a Greyhound. The dog stood at the glass door of the owner's part of the property; her ears perked up, her eyes fixed on me.

The property owner had a few dogs; they were fidgeting around, barking and jumping, but the Greyhound stood motionlessly like a statue, never taking her eyes off mine.

There was something magnetic in her gaze. I experienced a feeling I couldn't quite explain, and before I had a chance to figure it out, the property owner ushered the dogs away so that I could enter and get to rent the place.

I liked the place, but honestly, the Greyhound was the main reason I was drawn to renting it.

As I walked out after signing the lease, I turned around and saw the Greyhound back at the glass door, staring at me and wagging her tail, and I swear it looked like she was smiling.

For the rest of the evening, I couldn't get the gaze of that Greyhound out of my mind, so I was looking forward to moving in and meeting that incredible dog.

And so it began, five years of sharing the yard with Roxi, where I could play with her all I wanted, and our connection was so obvious that the landlady offered me to walk her too, take her to the park, or anywhere I wanted, and that I gladly did.

From the very beginning, I started noticing the moments when Roxi lay in the yard within close proximity to my whereabouts, following me with eyes full of such pure love that it often moved me to tears, especially at times when the rest of the world wasn't quite on the same page. It never occurred to me to ponder why this felt so familiar.

And then, on a rather distressful day, I was sitting on the low step outside of my front door, trying to catch some air and calm my nerves. I could see Roxi behind the closed glass doors. I heard her whimpering and scratching to come out, but I had no energy to let her out.

The landlady answered the dog's plea and opened the door. First, she rushed towards me but stopped abruptly, fixing her gaze on my eyes.

Roxi stood for a moment looking at me, then walked up to me slowly, pressed her chest into me, placed her head on my shoulder, and froze. I felt her heartbeat as I knew she could feel mine.

The hug! I gasped, wrapping my arms around her neck in disbelief. Lana?

As tears rolled down my face, I heard my landlady's voice saying: "I can't believe this. She doesn't hug anyone like this, not even me!"

Roxi died of cancer two years after I moved out.

PART THREE
The Hedgehog Lady

Back in 2010, when I was still living in New York City and my life was starting to change into what it is now, I signed up for a Life Coaching Course in California.

A friend who wanted to attend the course with me arranged for us to stay with someone she knew, who was also attending.

The strangest feeling came over me as we arrived at our hostess's place and met her. There was something about her and her round, hunched-over body, her small hands, dark beady eyes, and pointy nose.

There was something about her very presence that felt incredibly odd to me. It was a feeling I had never experienced before, and I couldn't quite place my finger on it.

In addition to that, everything inside our hostess's house was brown. The ceilings were low, the doorways were arched, brown curtains blocked the daylight, brown covers were on the beds, brown furniture stood in the living room, even the towels and the sheets were brown, and there was clutter everywhere.

To me, the place looked more like a storage space than a home. It felt strange, as if we were underground and had entered a den that was dug deep into the earth and stuffed to the brim.

The next day at the course, we did an exercise where we wrote down five repeating thoughts we commonly had daily.

When our hostess shared her thoughts, she herself was surprised to see that the predominant thoughts she had throughout her every day were about food. Her five predominant thoughts were breakfast, lunch, dinner, storage of leftovers, and getting more food.

When we talked later that evening, she shared that she had children but hadn't seen them since they were old enough to fend for themselves. According to her, this didn't bother her in the slightest, and from looking at her, it was obvious that it didn't.

The hostess just shrugged and said, "I had them; I fed them till they were old enough to feed themselves, and after that, my duties to them were complete."

Just like an animal, I thought, with the strangest feeling.

She must've picked up on this, as quite out of the blue the hostess proceeded to tell us the following.

Some years ago, she wanted to know about her past lives and why she felt so different from the rest of the people. For a reading, she chose to go to a Scientology institute.

As the Scientologists did their thing to read her past lives, they found themselves quite startled. To their great surprise, all they could see was the life of a hedgehog that got run over by a carriage.

This was where the reading came to a halt; as try as they might, they were unable to find anything else.

CHAPTER SIX
Theories and Conclusions

PART ONE
Cosmic Souls and the Three Stages of Human History

Those who remember making a choice to come to Earth from a different place in the cosmos often wonder why they didn't know that this place was a trap.

This question puzzled me as well, as I couldn't imagine agreeing to be used and recycled on Earth for centuries. Was there a "small print" in my agreement to come to Earth that I didn't notice? Try as I might, I just couldn't recall this part.

I received the answer in one of my private sessions.

We came in before the reincarnation cycle was in place; this is why we had no awareness of it.

According to the download I had, there were three stages of history on this planet. During the first two stages, Earth was "managed" by a different set of "owners"; human beings had all of their abilities intact, and their souls were free to come and go.

The soul entrapment system was created by the new handlers of Earth after they fought in space for the ownership of this territory and won.

They implemented the third stage of human history, installed the Matrix system, and the reincarnation cycle. These handlers are running this planet to this day.

All of this happened while the cosmic souls were already on Earth in flesh and bone. We did not find out about the newly-created entrapment system until our physical lives were over, and we faced the fact that we could no longer come and go as we used to.

PART TWO
Trauma by Design

The new owners of Earth didn't just change the systems here; they also changed the body vehicles that their subjects had to now occupy.

This is when the alterations of the human DNA took place, and our innate abilities were made dormant to ensure that the population of this planet was easy to control and manipulate.

You can find references to this in the brilliant work of Paul Wallis, "Escaping from Eden," where he shines the light on the whole process that, according to him, is very clearly laid out in The Book of Genesis.

But doing just that was not enough for the handlers. For their own energetic sustenance, they needed the loosh that humans produce due to suffering; and so, our physical brains were also changed.

The "downgraded" brain that the newly-modified human body was now equipped with had a couple of "convenient" new functions.

The first function of the new human brain was that of filtering out everything irrelevant to the immediate physical survival. This ensured that humans did not venture too far into any non-physical awareness but were now focused firmly and exclusively on the painful physicality of their existence.

Our present-day brain research confirms this unfortunate fact. It states that the human brain receives and is capable of processing 11 million bits of information per second, but our conscious minds can handle only 40 to 50 bits.

The second "convenient" new function of the human brain was the creation of the "subconscious" function, which hid the conditioning and removed the awareness of the behavioral patterns that resulted from traumas.

Losing conscious access to the subconscious space created a constant "blind spot" within human behavior, assuring recycling of the traumas generation after generation and thus continuous production of loosh for the handlers.

The origination of the traumas that to this day are passed on from one generation to the next began at the time of creation of the new human body vehicles.

The first "new humans" of that era were conditioned to view themselves as inferior to their creators; unworthy, undeserving, primitive, dirty, and guilty of their very existence.

Passed on from generation to generation ever since, this deliberately created conditioning is still within the core of most human traumas and behaviors.

PART THREE
Material Desires and Paying off Karma

Cut off from their higher essence and stuck within the "new" modified bodies that were now plugged into the Matrix system, human beings became blind, disconnected, and misguided, running in circles one lifetime after the next, in a perpetual state of longing for something they could no longer consciously recall.

New modified humans were created to be the workforce for the Matrix, and the Archons utilized the constant longing of the human souls to direct human attention towards physical desires and material gain that was now presented as the passage towards fulfillment.

Trapped within the limited awareness of purely physical existence, humans were now bound to spend their lives chasing after material fulfillment, while simultaneously being judged for doing so through religious and social beliefs.

It was a deliberately generated "catch 22" where the sense of guilt for the very thing we were programmed to do was constantly reinforced, never to let the humans forget how "imperfect" and "undeserving" they were.

Then came the teachings about overcoming desires and "paying off Karma." Interestingly enough, the "Karma" that we now had to "pay off" had everything to do with a person trying to find happiness through fulfilling their human desires.

Do you see how clever the system is in setting the trap for the souls?

First, we are conditioned to seek fulfillment in material desires and thus serve the Matrix. Then in the afterlife, we are judged for doing so, and after that, we are sent back to Earth to continue doing the same exact thing life after life.

Human fixation on the fulfillment of material desires gets imprinted so deeply that it is carried into the afterlife too, and the Archons utilize it in their convincing tactics. A promise of riches or happy romantic unions in the next life makes human subjects susceptible to accepting the next cycle of reincarnation.

What we are taught to perceive as "Soul Karma," in reality, has nothing to do with the soul itself and everything to do with the traumatic and artificial conditioning humans undergo while living within the Matrix system, and the behaviors that result from the above.

Those humans who were traumatized to the highest degree but had no awareness of what was motivating their actions due to the lack of access to the hidden subconscious mind, acted unconsciously and did not select paths of integrity when seeking fulfillment of their material desires.

These are the choices that they will be judged for during the life review, but these were not the choices that their souls made.

None of the choices related to the material existence on Earth are made by our souls.

Our souls are pure, infinite, and content within their core. From where I stand, there is no such thing as "Soul Karma."

Humans are being punished and judged for acting out of the very conditioning that was instilled into us deliberately by the Archons. This is nothing more than being judged for simply being a human and told that we have to "pay that off," which by design is impossible, and the Akashic records are there to keep the score of every individual action.

The longer we are on Earth and the more experiences we have as a physical human, the more "Karma" we "accumulate."

I find it ironic that the whole "paying off Karma" system is set up exactly like a credit card debt.

Those of us who manage to recall some of our past lives try to work on the issues we become aware of, which makes no difference for our future incarnations due to the mind-wipe between lives.

The process could be likened to making a "minimum payment" now and then, but the so-called "Karmic debt" continues to grow.

The majority of the Earth's population lives in complete oblivion about the system and its "Karmic demands" upon them, all the way until they are facing the handlers during the life review after death. This is when the guilt instilled into our very essence is triggered and we agree to go back and "do better next time."

In reality, no one is "paying off" anything. It is all a big hoax used to convince the humans to take more incarnations on Earth.

PART FOUR
Overcoming Desires

Overcoming material human desires is presented in Eastern traditional teachings as a big part of the process of enlightenment. Letting go of all material desires promises us the attainment of higher states of consciousness. The masses look up to those who live ascetic lives in ashrams and monasteries of all traditions.

My response to the above is that it is not uncommon for the human mind to confuse the effect with the cause, and in this case, as in many others, we got everything backward. Here is what I mean by this.

The body vehicle is wired into the Matrix system through its needs, desires, and thoughts by design. The biological brain serves as an antenna, constantly receiving the "incoherent noise" from the Matrix and "survival" states of unprocessed traumas, both our own and other people's, that we experience as "thoughts."

The nagging feeling of something unfulfilled within us is present for the majority of the Earth's population, and we are misguided to seek that "something" through the fulfillment of material and physical desires.

Engaging in spiritual practices like the Cosmic Cobra Breath and deep nighttime meditations helps to gain control over your body and the biological "brain-computer." It leads to experiencing the state of omnipresence, which is the "missing piece" that we lost after the modification of our brains by the Archons.

Finding this "missing piece" and experiencing the true essence of our souls gives us the state of the deepest fulfillment there is. We realize what it was that we were longing for and trying to find through the fulfillment of material desires, and the fixation on material desires melts away like ice cream on a summer day.

Repressing desires we are programmed to have by sheer willpower, just because we believe that we should have none, is a futile and challenging task for most, and the result does not work long-term.

We can experience an illusion that it's working for a while, but it usually backfires after some time; thus, all the lawsuits and sex scandals of the modern-day "spiritual teachers."

Desires lessen, "dry up," and "fall off" quite naturally once we experience and embody the all-encompassing state of being, the Absolute, where everything is present and nothing is missing.

Left brain logic lingers to remind us why we need this or that while in the physical, so we keep going through the motions to take care of the needs of our everyday physical lives, but we arrive at a state where we no longer experience the constant yearning for something unattainable.

A great sense of inner peace follows.

PART FIVE
Learning Lessons and Soul Evolution Theory

Many of us have adopted a comforting belief that we are on Earth to learn lessons, to contribute to Source Consciousness, and to propel our soul's evolution. This idea certainly feels better than believing that we have been trapped and manipulated into the whole thing, but is it true?

I tend to disagree, as anyone who has ever experienced their innate soul's pure and infinite state knows that the soul requires no evolution.

Our soul is an all-encompassing field of energy that already contains within itself all the lessons, all the answers, and all the consciousness, both cosmic and human.

The completeness and perfection of our true soul, which we all have within our core, is unparalleled and does not require any additional input from any experience.

Regarding "learning lessons" on Earth and thus contributing to the Source Consciousness, here is one more perspective that I can offer in addition to all of the information I have already shared in this chapter.

We are told and want to believe that we are unique snowflakes and that our human experiences on Earth are rare and special.

But how many variations of the human experience are there within each era and each individual soul group that keeps incarnating together? Truth be told, not so many.

Sometimes, during personal sessions, week after week, I am astonished to hear the same exact story coming from people who, on paper, have nothing in common at all.

These people are of different ages and different genders; they live on different continents and speak different languages, and yet their stories are nearly identical.

There are only so many variations of the human experience that exist within the Matrix system or were programmed into the simulation.

Even if we still want to believe that after centuries and centuries of identical human cycles, the all-encompassing Field of Divine Source still requires input from our stories, I have no doubt that it has already seen it all by now.

There is only one way that the idea of updating "the Source" with our experiences could possibly be true. And that is if what's referred to as "Source" is quite literally the "*source code*" of the backend AI software that generates and runs the simulation for the Matrix system.

In this case, the Akashic records of human behavior continuously feed the database and serve to upgrade this software so that a more current and updated simulation can be generated both in the afterlife realm and also on Earth.

PART SIX
Turn Away from the Light Theory

There are theories out there now suggesting that if we want to get out of the afterlife entrapment system, then at the moment of death, when we see the tunnel of white light, we need to turn away from it and go into the purple light or any other color light. We are also told that to avoid the afterlife dimension, we simply need to declare that we want to go home. I find both suggestions flawed.

Firstly, if you are facing the tunnel of white light, you will likely not stand a chance of avoiding it. The white light tunnel is so strong that it will vacuum you up like a particle of dust.

You might recall the story about the blue light tunnel and the ETs present at the time of a person's passing that I shared in "LEAVING THE TRAP." I posit that the blue, purple, or any other color tunnel of light will do the same as the tunnel of white light, except that it will "spit you out" in a different area of the reincarnation cycle.

Declaring "I want to go home" puts you in a disempowered position. To whom are you declaring this exactly? To the trickster handlers of the reincarnation machine? Good luck with that.

If you are talking to the handlers, it is too late for you already. They can read you like an open book and easily show you all kinds of places to choose from that will feel like "home" to you, but none of these places will be outside the entrapment system.

Feeling trapped yet? Getting out of the reincarnation system isn't a game, and certainly not a fair game either, and the Archons know exactly what to do to keep you.

Here is the solution that I offer, and I do not tire of repeating it over and over. Wake up your Kundalini energy and use it as rocket fuel to fly out of the top of your head and bust out of the dimensions of the Matrix.

Do this over and over so that you can teach yourself while still alive how to operate your non-physical form, your spirit body, and how to direct it past the astral afterlife dimension straight into the True Void.

You will be pulled back to the body again and again while the body is alive, but you will develop the skill required to exit the system, and you will be able to utilize this skill at the moment of passing. This is your ticket to freedom.

Developing this skill will require patience, discipline, and effort, but if you persevere, at least you'll give yourself a choice.

CHAPTER SEVEN
Practices and Side-Effects

PART ONE
Why Do the Practices?

The practices that I recommend are geared towards training oneself to quantum travel/quantum jump out of dimensions of the Matrix, bypassing the entire afterlife dimension altogether. This, in my opinion, is the only method that could potentially guarantee that you will not be trapped again.

These practices are very effective yet minimal enough for any person with discipline to engage in every day.

The main objective of these practices is *to develop the skill of handling your spirit form while still alive* and to open the door out of the reincarnation cycle and the Matrix structures and back into the Quantum Field of the Absolute.

In other words, if you choose to practice what I recommend, you will be training for your final departure.

The Matrix and the handlers count on us lacking inner discipline, being weak, and unable to lift our gaze from the dramas of our daily survival.

These are the qualities that the Matrix system supports and cultivates within the human race, as these qualities keep the humans controllable while feeding and sustaining the system itself.

By reviving and claiming the willpower to overcome our Matrix-serving body and get up in the middle of the night for our practice, to sit through it no matter what, and to maintain our practice daily, we overcome the shackles and create a different choice for ourselves.

This is something that is required for our overcoming the system's control over our bodies, minds, lives, and deaths. Finding and reclaiming this inner power is the first step towards our liberation and a prerequisite to exiting the system.

You absolutely must find this within yourself, as waiting for the "saviors" has proven futile so far. Humanity has been waiting for the saviors throughout our entire history, but we are still pretty much where we were before.

Few illuminated souls did show up in human form (Jesus, Buddha) and what did humanity do? We killed them or ignored their teachings in favor of continuing to dig through piles of our daily chores.

Many ideas of alien saviors are circulating nowadays, suggesting that the aliens will show up and change everything for us or take us away in their ships. We are told that they will take down the entrapment system and liberate humanity. Some are even saying that it had already been done.

If these stories were true, it would be fantastic indeed. Otherwise, I see that the ideas of the external saviors, be they enlightened Masters or ETs, only contribute to keeping the human race at the level of powerless sheep, passively counting on the shepherds to show up and take care of everything.

As much as I too would like to find out that these alien savior stories are actually true, I still encourage you to take your power back into your own hands, follow the preparation steps that I suggest both in this book and in "LEAVING THE TRAP," and train yourselves while still alive to deal with, or better off, to bypass the system of reincarnation.

If, on the way out of the body at death, you discover that the astral plane and the reincarnation cycle had indeed been dismantled, that surely will be a happy moment. But if you find that the contrary is true, which unfortunately appears to be a more likely scenario, you will be prepared.

PART TWO
Waking up Your Kundalini

The practices that I recommend are intended for waking up and gaining control over your Kundalini energy, which, in a nutshell, is the "rocket fuel" that can propel your spirit form out of the Matrix structure. Kundalini energy is a manifestation of Prana, a universal life force or vital energy that flows through every physical body.

Many stories of the dangers of awakening the Kundalini energy circulate among spiritual circles and the common population.

Although some of the stories of the side effects that occurred due to careless or mindless practices that forced the Kundalini energy to awaken in mentally unstable or unprepared subjects might be true, I posit that this is no different than mentally unprepared people having freak-out episodes with psychedelics.

I still suggest that the main purpose of these stories is the scare tactics to keep the general population away from attempting to awaken the energy that will restore access to their subconscious minds and innate abilities.

In nearly six years of attending Dr. Joe Dispenza's workshops with thousands of others, where Kundalini awakening was a part of the process for many, I have not witnessed even one freak-out episode.

That said, it is important to know that Kundalini energy is a powerful force that is a part of you, and its awakening is to be approached with respect.

If the fear is strong within you and you cannot handle yourself when things become unpredictable, strange, and intense, then this path is not for you or you need to seek out a teacher who will walk you towards your Kundalini awakening at a slow pace.

In one of my early experiences with the Kundalini movement, the energy awakened and shot both up and down my spine. The sheer force of it blinded me with fireworks inside my brain, and also broke two wooden boards of the bed underneath me. I was sitting on pillows on top of the mattress, and although I wasn't moving at all, the boards that held the mattress cracked in half directly underneath my root center.

It is quite apparent to me that when the Kundalini awakens and rushes up the spine, lighting up the upper chakras, the brain, and the spine from within, *it burns away the artificially installed "dumbing down" mechanism* that was applied to the human race by our most recent handlers.

There was a time when humans had all their abilities intact. We knew our true non-physical essence and could peer into the Cosmos.

This was threatening for the Archons as the humans were as powerful as them. So the decision was made to put an end to it and send a "dark cloud" over the human eyes to remove our ability for the higher vision.

This I read in Paul Wallis's book "Escaping from Eden". He tells us that the description of the process can be found in The Book of Genesis.

What he says makes perfect sense to me. If we are always a part of Source, the Omnipresent Absolute, why are most people not aware of it?

Our abilities and our access to the truth are within our "dormant" DNA, but the DNA wasn't always dormant. It was made dormant by design in order to keep the human workforce controllable and easy to manipulate.

If all of us had awakened our Kundalini, burnt away the "blindfold," and regained access to the true essence of ourselves, no one would be left to serve the Archons.

Those who endure severe brain traumas often tap into their abilities as a result. These abilities go away if a person's brain fully recovers. Something is seriously wrong with this picture, don't you think?

I promise you that through determination, Cosmic Cobra Breath, and mid-sleep meditations, we can reactivate ourselves to the degree that allows us to return to Source; to know the Absolute; to have our innate abilities restored once again; and to become a liberated sovereign human, all of which is our birthright.

PART THREE
Eastern Traditions vs. the Truth

Traditional Eastern teachings tell us that we can only experience Samadhi, tap into the Field of Omnipresence or enter the True Void after we let go of our human self completely. The idea of doing this first is often presented as a requirement in order to enter the Absolute. This places additional mental obstacles in the way of a normal human being who wants to have the experience but also wants to keep living their regular everyday life.

Many traditional teachings require their students to stay at the ashrams or monasteries, which confuses many people into thinking that in order to gain access to the Absolute and their true essence, they have to give up their regular lives and choose one or the other: to either be spiritual or to be able to maintain their regular lives.

Although, personally, I would love to be able to give up my regular life and dedicate as much time as I want to breathwork and meditation, for everyone else who simply wants to get out of the reincarnation cycle, giving up your everyday life is not required at all.

All of the traditional notions that I shared above couldn't be farther from the truth. In this, as in most other areas of human "expertise," the fascinating human tendency of confusing the cause with the effect or the chicken with the egg is the most apparent.

Not only that, but these teachings yet again reinforce the idea that we are "imperfect" and "undeserving" and that we have to change ourselves completely in order to become "worthy" of experiencing what in truth already is and always had been our own.

My own experience and the experiences of many of those who practice the same thing had been so that no lengthy preparation is required for Kundalini Awakening and the quantum jump into the True Void.

What is required is the right technique, and the Cosmic Cobra Breath *is* the right technique; the inner determination and the discipline to do your practice every night; and also the ability to handle yourself when things start getting more and more intense, so that you endure and sit through the wild explosion of the awakening Kundalini energy within you, till it takes you out of your body; rather than getting scared and giving up at the first hint of this unfamiliar discomfort.

And then it happens. You enter the True Void, and all of your human self, your body, your mind, your personality, all of who and what you are, your entire humanness dissolves completely, and you experience yourself as the very fabric that your pure and infinite soul is made of.

You return to the unformed in the state of High Samadhi or within the True Void. You experience yourself as the primordial consciousness of everything and nothing; the perfection of the Absolute, of which you are a part.

And you don't have to do a thing to deserve this. This experience is what alters your life, your mind, and your essence forever.

One time is plenty to do just that, and many give up right there, thinking that they have attained enlightenment, and it's a done deal.

In truth, if you continue your practice past your very first experience, you will develop the skill of taking yourself out of the body and into the True Void *as often as you wish*.

You will pave the way into the Absolute by will, not by accident; and you will find that your experiences and the freedom that comes with them will deepen and expand with time. This I can guarantee.

PART FOUR
Variations of the Cosmic Cobra Breath

Mystical traditions worldwide have been utilizing different styles of breathwork to induce altered states of consciousness from the beginning of time. The proper technique to start training for your final hour is "The Cosmic Cobra Breath" or "Tantric Kriya Kundalini Pranayam."

This technique is considered to be a safe way of awakening your Kundalini energy as it doesn't allow the energy to move until your system prepares itself through regular repetition of the practice.

This is very important to know for those who might be in a hurry "to get there" and those feeling a bit nervous about starting due to all of the scare tactics related to the Kundalini awakening.

Although I feel that teaching the Cosmic Cobra Breath in a book is inappropriate, I will still give you some useful tips below.

The Cosmic Cobra Breath is an ancient psycho-spiritual breathwork technique practiced in nearly all mystical traditions around the world.

It is believed to first have been offered to humanity by Babaji and then incorporated into these mystical systems.

There is a Sufi Cobra Breath, an Egyptian Cobra Breath, a Kriya Yoga Cobra Breath, a Tantric Kriya Cobra Breath, and a Taoist Cobra Breath, to name a few.

This breathwork is known for its life-changing powers and can be applied in many different ways. The outcome depends on the initial intent of the practitioner.

Dr. Joe Dispenza, whose work I praise and highly recommend as it changed my life and helped me become who I am today, teaches a few variations of the Cosmic Cobra Breath.

My first introduction to this breathwork came through Dr. Dispenza's powerful work, and I always give him credit for this introduction.

Master Teacher Jeffrey Boehme, Ramtha's School of Enlightenment, and I all teach variations of the Cosmic Cobra Breath, but the applications of this ancient yogic technique vary vastly depending on the objective of the teacher.

Through ten years of practice and much trial and error, I have developed my own variations of the Cosmic Cobra Breath, incorporating additional subtle elements that worked the best for me.

Throughout my practice, I discovered that the intention and style of The Cosmic Cobra Breath, coupled with the techniques I now teach, allows the practitioner to leave their body at will and find themselves in the primordial field of the unmanifest beyond all form.

This field of the True Void, as I now call it, is outside of the structures of the Matrix and the reincarnation systems.

Once I made this discovery, *I connected the process of exiting the reincarnation cycle with training oneself to go out of the body at will by utilizing The Cosmic Cobra Breath.*

None of the practitioners I mentioned above or currently know of focus on the same objective.

For example, how Dr. Dispenza utilizes The Cosmic Cobra Breath has an entirely different objective than mine. His guided meditations keep the mind of the practitioner constantly engaged, which works brilliantly for his objective, but does not allow the meditator's mind to cease activity and settle into complete silence.

From these standpoints alone, the concepts that we teach and the applications of the Cosmic Cobra Breath couldn't be more different.

But suppose you are Dr. Dispenza's student, as I was for many years too, and have already learned the variations of the Cosmic Cobra Breath that he teaches. In that case you can continue using his breathwork techniques as they are sufficient to be practiced in preparation for exiting the reincarnation cycle.

You will just need to align yourself with a different objective.

Here is how to do it. Listen to my interviews on YouTube for free, read my book "LEAVING THE TRAP," and create a meditation playlist with no verbal guidance past the breathwork segment, or start practicing in silence.

If this is too much for you to figure out on your own, you can seek me out as a teacher to receive guidance through my Workshops.

PART FIVE
Mid-Sleep Meditation

There is a reason why monks of all traditions begin their practices in the darkness in the middle of the night before dawn. The hours between one and four in the morning are considered to be the "sacred hours" when access to the Divine is direct. Scriptures of all religious traditions support this notion.

From a scientific point of view, these are exactly the hours when we have access to the beneficial chemistry that the brain produces while we sleep during the night, which is simply not available during the day.

Getting up mid-sleep and practicing the Cosmic Cobra Breath or Tantric Kriya Kundalini Pranayam between the hours of one and four in the morning, followed by sitting with heart-opening meditative music, is the technique that leads to Kundalini Awakening, quantum travel, soul liberation, and ultimately allows you to hop out of the reincarnation cycle at the end of your life.

Can you do this practice in the morning, during the day, or at the end of your day? You sure can, but you will not get the same result.

If you prefer to start doing the practice in the morning, make sure to add the grounding practice immediately after to regain full physical focus for your day (see Part Seven, "Grounding Practice"). Know that as soon as the first rays of daylight hit your eyeballs, the chemistry in the brain will change, and you will lose access to the chemistry that assists your out-of-body experiences.

Doing the practice in the evening, right before you go to sleep, will give you interesting dreams and could be ok at the beginning if you are successful with it.

Be mindful not to try doing the practice if you had alcohol, if your stomach is still full after dinner, or if you just had sex. Here is why.

If you had alcohol, your frequency has been lowered, and your focus is off, so you're not going anywhere anyway, plus you might have additional unpleasant side effects.

If your stomach is still full and your body is utilizing all of its energy to digest your dinner, you simply won't have access to the energy you are trying to wake up. Digestion will interfere with the energy movement, and doing the breathwork where you are squeezing the abdomen on a full stomach might actually make you throw up.

If you had sex before starting your practice, you quite literally just let your Kundalini energy that you're trying to move into the upper centers be drained out during your sexual activity, and your tank is empty, so to speak.

The other drawback of trying to do your practice at the end of the day is that you might be tired after a long day, and your mind is still wired up with everything that happened earlier. You might start the practice and find that you are lacking focus and are overpowered by your mind's insistent chatter, and then you might simply fall asleep due to sheer exhaustion.

The end of the day is really not the best time for this practice.

Neither is the middle of the day, even if you do have such availability, due to your left brain being in overdrive. Your intent to get out of the body will be interfered with by the brain activity that will continue to bring your mind's attention to the events of your life.

That said, starting your practice at any time is still better than not starting it at all.

100% of my students who first did the practice during the day and then switched to practicing mid-sleep reported that the effects were amplified significantly and that they could finally reach the desired outcome.

Here is how to do it.

Go to bed early, set the alarm to get up between 1 and 4 am to do the practice in the middle of the night, then sleep for a few more hours before getting up for your day.

We call this "mid-sleep meditation" because you sleep for some time before you do it, and then sleep some more afterward.

As "impossible" as your brain might tell you this sounds, this is what I've been doing every night for the last ten years, so I can promise you from experience that the body adjusts to the new routine and the whole thing doesn't appear so "challenging" anymore.

Do not be concerned with the myth of "not getting enough sleep." Even if you do not go to bed early and still get up to do the meditation, you will be less tired the next day than if you just sleep through it.

The practice rejuvenates the body way more than sleep does. You will get healthier and have more vitality if you do the mid-sleep practice than if you don't.

I went over all the details of my personal mid-sleep meditation practice in "LEAVING THE TRAP," but many people missed this part or were unable to apply it to themselves, so here is the same information in as clear a format as I can master. The information below will overlap with other parts of this chapter.

Here is what you need:

- Strong intent and willingness to do your practice no matter what (the end goal is massive!)
- Attitude of awe, playfulness, and curiosity (this isn't yet another "chore" but a potential gateway into the biggest adventure of your life!)
- The right spot for your practice (see Part Six, "Dealing With Side-Effects")
- The alarm clock that makes a gentle sound and has red color digits and light. Get rid

of all alarm clocks that have blue, white, or yellow digits. Even the little light that they emit will interfere with your brain chemistry. Only red spectrum light doesn't.

- A flashlight with a red color setting. Use it to go to the bathroom, light your way around the room when you move to your designated spot, and point it at the screen of the device that you will use to play music.

- A blindfold. Complete darkness is crucial, so get the eye mask that has the black-out technology. I use the mask made by "Mindfold."

- A meditative music playlist that's at least two hours long. See my remarks about music vs. silence below.

- If you opt for a playlist, which is a good idea at the beginning, your playlist should start with a short 3-4 min track for while you are settling into your spot, followed by a 15 min track to keep time during breathwork; followed by at least two hours of meditative music.

- A dedicated device to play your music if you opt to use music. Set the device to dark mode, turn off wi-fi, and set the volume and the playlist to be ready. Do all of this before you go to bed. I have a dedicated device for the practice to avoid doing this every evening. Put your eye mask on, point the red light to the screen, click play, shut the lid, or flip the device face down. Do not linger looking at the screen; the light of the screen will mess with your brain chemistry.

Having a pre-recorded breathwork track and music to keep time during your meditation is a good idea at the beginning, as many find this helpful. However, becoming accustomed to having the music could interfere with developing the ability to do the Cosmic Cobra Breath and meditation without the assistance of a recording or any music at all.

What helps with developing this skill is first doing the Cosmic Cobra Breath during the day when your left brain is active and you can pay attention to what you are doing. Making it *automatic* will take *one week* of daily practice. Taking this skill into your nighttime meditations will then be a piece of cake.

Ideally, we want to learn to facilitate our out-of-body experiences and quantum travel into the

True Void without any music at all. Think about it: chances are there won't be a pre-recorded soundtrack at the moment of your final departure.

PART SIX
Dealing with Side-Effects

Although I posit that awakening your Kundalini energy through the practice of the Cosmic Cobra Breath is not nearly as "dangerous" as the scare tactics want us to believe, and your energy will not move until your system has prepared itself through repetition of the practice, there are definitely side-effects I want you to be aware of that accompany the process.

Here on Earth, you come equipped with the mind-ego-body team that is quite literally plugged into the Matrix system and deliberately wired to prevent you from venturing away from the body and discovering the truth.

The body is also equipped with the fear of darkness, natural for the type of beings whose sensory organs were not made to function well in the dark.

The mind-body-ego structure is there to serve both the system and your physical survival for the benefit of the system. Its job is to keep your body safe and your physical desires intact and to also ensure that you remain within the constraints of physical reality.

Although our mind-body-ego team is quite useful when it comes to our everyday lives, as it keeps us fed, clothed, and physically well, it is programmed to perceive our getting out of the body as a direct threat to its very existence; and thus all kinds of weirdness geared towards preventing you from going anywhere might occur once you try.

And the strongest of these things is **fear**.

Mental interference, fear of the Void

- If you have an overwhelming darkness phobia, the practices I teach are not for you.

- If, same as millions of people on this planet, you've been conditioned to believe that "Hell" is the "utter *darkness* where there will be weeping and gnashing of teeth" and you take the word "darkness" literally, the practices I teach are not for you, as you will most definitely misinterpret the black ocean of The Void and freak-out.

- If you have a strong phobia of going out of body, and the mere thought of it puts you in panic, the practices I teach are not for you. Your identification with the physical body is too strong and you are simply not ready.

- If you've experienced the Void during an NDE or otherwise, but felt "bored" because "nothing was happening", the practices I teach are not for you. Your ego-based perception of reality is too strong. Feel free to allow yourself to enjoy a few more life cycles on Earth, where action is always present in abundance.

Fear isn't as pronounced with astral projecting, which occurs as a result of very deep relaxation. At the beginning of your astral projecting, you might experience gentle vibrations and then find yourself in a different part of Earth-related reality or simply standing in your room looking at your body.

I do not tire of saying that we are not training to astral project for two reasons. Astral projecting is way more dangerous than quantum travel.

The astral realm is full of entities and spirits that don't hesitate to interfere or mess with you and can also follow you back into your body.

However, the main reason not to astral project is that the astral dimensions are a part of the Matrix and the reincarnation systems, so astral projecting defeats our efforts to leave these systems behind.

It is worth mentioning that as gentle as astral projecting is on the body compared to Quantum travel, the fear of separation from the body still might kick in, in which case most people will interrupt the experience and pull back into the body.

Compared to astral projecting, Quantum travel triggered by the Kundalini fire is a whole different experience.

There is nothing gentle about it, not at the beginning, anyway.

When starting your Cobra Breath and mid-sleep meditation practice, your main objective will be to learn how to handle yourself, your fear of physical discomfort, your mental resistance and the fear of the unknown.

The first experience of Kundalini awakening is *very intense* and you will need to be ready to let go of control, overcome fear and allow things to unfold as they may.

Consecutive experiences of Kundalini movement will become less and less intense until all intensity will eventually subside.

Think about the whole thing, like trying alcohol, pot, or psychedelics for the first time. People are not doing these to feel the same way as before. They don't know exactly how they are going to feel, but they know that their physical and mental states will get altered, and very possibly significantly so, yet they go for it regardless.

Adopt the same attitude towards your Kundalini awakening.

Bringing the attitude of curiosity, excitement, and a sense of awe into your practice is also very helpful. Play with it, and be curious to explore! You literally have no idea what might occur in each one of your mid-sleep meditations. And if nothing occurs, tomorrow is another day!

When your Kundalini energy finally moves up the spine, your body will feel like it is on fire.

Sweat will be rolling down your body. You might involuntarily shake, move, or scream right as the indescribable fireworks go off inside your head. You will blow out of the top of your head like a rocket, and then everything will get quiet and still, and you will no longer be in your body.

This is exactly what we are training for! It will be your first experience of the objective that we are working towards: your first quantum jump.

If your quantum jump landed you in the True Void and you suddenly found yourself in the "Black Ocean of nothing," – congratulations! You have arrived! Most people experience indescribable bliss, peace, and perfection, and they also experience blissful things that words cannot describe.

But if you find that you are feeling eerie, which happens once in a while at first, do your best to keep your system calm. If brain activity is still there, tell yourself: "I'm okay," and remain still.

Do not try to look for "yourself" as a human within this vast black space. *You aren't there as a human but as the base fabric of your soul.*

If your system remains calm, or after it calms down again, you will feel the peace and the perfection of this primordial field and experience yourself as a part of the consciousness of everything.

And if the built-in fear response was so strong that it pulled you back into your body, don't beat yourself up: tomorrow is another night to do it again and again and again until you become comfortable with the whole experience and are able to feel the silent bliss of the True Void.

The best way to deal with the built-in fear is to prepare yourself mentally before you even start your meditations, to coach yourself to know that you will be totally fine both during and after these experiences.

Once you get over the initial "hump" of fear, you will know firsthand how limitless you are!

Make sure that during the entire process, you are sitting up against the wall or against something large enough to support your body and your head.

My favorite story of the year was about the person who tried doing their Cosmic Cobra

Breath while sitting on top of the toilet with the lid closed.

They thought it was a cool and private place and that the seat supported their spine, so they sat there and went for it.

Later that night, they woke up on the floor in their bathroom next to the toilet. As funny as it sounds now, the toilet is not a good spot to do your practice.

I also do not recommend doing your practice lying down, sitting in a chair, or on a small stool that has no back.

Do not do your practice on the edge of the bed or a couch where the mattress or the pillows will sink underneath you and your spine will curve.

You will need a solid foundation behind and underneath you to keep your spine straight and your body supported.

And in case you do launch, which will feel very much like a "blackout" of the body with your consciousness fully awake and having the experience of your life, do not sit next to any lamps, candles, sharp objects, large crystals, or sharp edges anywhere around you.

I believe the best spot for your breath work and meditation practice is on the floor against the wall, ideally in the same room where you sleep, with pillows underneath and behind you.

Your "launch" will not happen on the first night. And depending on what your system can handle, it might not even happen for a few years.

But as soon as you start your practice, you will begin experiencing side effects, which will be your confirmation that your practice is working.

Remember that the symptoms are only strong at the beginning, but most of these symptoms will subside after you've conquered your body and mind, and practiced for some time.

Remember that the practice of the Cosmic Cobra Breath and mid-sleep meditation is by no means bad for your health. Quite the contrary, your health and general state of well-being will improve as a result of this practice.

Here are the side effects that you might or might not experience once you start doing the Cosmic Cobra Breath.

- Mental interference: fidgeting about the details of the set-up; thoughts of having no time or being too tired; having to use the restroom or move due to being uncomfortable; attention wandering onto the sounds, temperature, or the environment in the room; or onto a sudden pain in some part of your body. The variations are endless. But all of it is your ego-mind trying to prevent you from doing your practice.

- Fear to start, to go deep, or to repeat the next night

- Dizziness

- Trembling or involuntary shaking of your legs, shoulders, or your entire body.

- Swirling in the stomach

- Nausea, feeling like you are about to throw up (you won't. This is not very common unless your stomach is still full or you had alcohol earlier)

- Feeling like you are about to pass out (it's working!)

- Rapid or "loud" heartbeat (this is your heart receiving extra energy, nothing to be concerned about for most people. I had a minor heart condition when I started, but nothing happened to me except that the heart condition went away. However, if you do have a serious heart condition, please be mindful of it and proceed with caution)

- Involuntary movement of the hands, shoulders, legs, or the head

- Feeling pressure inside or on top of your head

- Head rolling back (head support is crucial!)

- Heat, sweat

- Making involuntary sounds

- Sense of disconnect from "yourself"

- Lost memories coming up

- Tears, sadness

- Feeling out of focus or unusually sensitive the next day (see the next part about a grounding practice).

Our individual side effects may vary, but the list above covers the most common ones I am aware of.

I know only one way to deal with the side effects: ignore them and sit through them, as they will completely disappear or diminish within the same meditation or eventually.

If you think that these side-effects are too much to bear, think about physical, mental and emotional discomforts that we endure on Earth for decades, day after day, life after life throughout the entirety of our incarnate existence. This really puts things in perspective.

In the beginning, I experienced all of the above, but my intent to continue with the practice and my curiosity for the mystical experiences was stronger than anything my mind or my body could do to make me stop. And then, eventually, all interference went away.

As I previously mentioned, I first learned a variation of the Cosmic Cobra Breath at one of

Dr. Joe Dispenza's early workshops. He did not mention any potential side-effects, but he gave us scientific explanations about the mechanics of what happens in the body when we do this practice.

If this is something that resonates with you and you are interested in knowing the scientific details of what you are doing, please refer to Dr. Dispenza's brilliant material, read his books, or attend his events. All that he offers is beyond fantastic from many standpoints.

After I learned the breath-work at the workshop in 2010, I immediately started doing it completely on my own every day, and nothing bad happened to me. Only incredible things happened. I wrote about many of them earlier in this book.

*Let go of the fear and know, to the bottom of your heart, that by definition, this practice cannot bring anything bad into your life. What it **can** bring you is a ticket to your soul freedom.*

Let your intent to liberate yourself through doing the practice be stronger than anything your mind, body, ego, or scare tactics can come up with to derail you.

Take charge of your choices and know that as uncomfortable as the whole thing might be at the beginning, the goal you are working towards is massive, and it is worth enduring all and every sort of physical and mental discomfort.

PART SEVEN
Grounding Practice

If your mid-sleep practice is working, you might find yourself out of focus the next day or feeling a bit more sensitive than usual. This is quite common.

Your overall frequency will increase due to your mid-sleep practice, which will affect your physical density. As time goes by, you will get used to your new state of not being so dense in 3D anymore.

Nothing is better than a grounding practice to assist you with this side effect.

Longer is better, but 15 minutes every morning will do the trick, 10 if you are "too busy."

If your environment and the weather permits go outside, sit in the sun, put your bare feet on the ground, and bring your full attention to the small details of nature around you. Get your left brain in gear by paying attention to the smells, the colors, and the intricacy of everything around you. Watch the dogs or the birds, the cats or the ants, or whatever living creatures you have around you and pay attention to their behavior.

This will connect you with the Earth's magnetic field and pull you back into the body, making it easier to focus on whatever you need to do in your life each day.

If access to nature is not there, get a grounding mat, put your feet on it for 10-15 minutes every morning, and simply sit closely observing every detail of your room, your house plants, or your pets. Do not, I beg you, start checking your phone first thing in the morning while sitting on a grounding mat.

Getting grounding sheets for your bed is also not a bad idea.

If you venture into your day and are still feeling out of focus, eat something hearty. Digesting heavy foods requires a lot of energy and it will drop your frequency and make you feel more "physical".

For example, eating organic meat grounds you back into the body almost instantly.

There are many recommendations about grounding products and practices on the Internet;

feel free to do your research and choose what works best for you, but if you are doing your nightly practice, do not skip the grounding. It will make a big difference for your daily life.

PART EIGHT
The True Void vs. Dimensions of the Matrix

Similarly to a video game where the environment within the game mimics real environments and terrains but is generated by the game itself, the Matrix simulation has generated a false presentation of everything organic. There is a mini-cosmos within the astral plane, a simulation of the True Light, and also a simulation of the True Void.

If your nighttime practices are working, you will soon start having mystical experiences and OBEs.

When going out of the body, it is important to be aware of what to look out for, just to know whether you have broken free or are still within the dimensions of the Matrix.

Here are a few recommendations based on my own experiences and experiences of numerous others who wrote to me over the course of the year.

Many have experienced coming out of the body and immediately encountering some sort of a being or beings who tried to interact with them, answering their quest for "truth," "show" them the "truth," or direct them to "the truth."

Some of the people who were specifically seeking the Void were directed into a dark space, which these people interpreted as "The Void," but they did not see it until the beings showed it to them during the interactions.

The beings in these stories ranged from extraterrestrials to Saints to passed-on grandmothers, completely unknown human-looking beings, and beings of white or blue light. The variations of the beings people experienced were endless, but the scenario of being intercepted as soon as out of the body was the same.

Many people experienced themselves as some sort of a being or form, ranging from a glowing humanoid form to a light sphere or an orb.

In most of these cases, people found themselves out of the body spontaneously or while lying down and deeply relaxing. This tells me they were astral projecting and did not quantum travel.

One person shared that she did manage to come out of the top of her head at the beginning of her Cosmic Cobra Breath practice but was still immediately intercepted by a spirit telling her only to do one of these breaths per session.

This tells me that although the woman managed to come out of the body in the way conducive to quantum travel, aka, out of the top of the head vs. slowly vibrating out of the body while relaxing, she still didn't go far enough, or did not generate enough life-force/Kundalini energy momentum to bust out of the astral realm.

Here is how to tell if you are still within the dimensions of the Matrix or managed to break free.

If you come out of the body and are intercepted by any sort of beings – you are within dimensions of the Matrix.

If you see yourself as any sort of form, be that a light form, glowing orb, or otherwise – you are within dimensions of the Matrix.

If you went through a tunnel of light on the way out of the body, right before you encountered the beings or experienced yourself as a light form, you are out of body within dimensions of the Matrix.

If you are seeing colors, light, glow, radiance, otherworldly-looking terrains, or heavenly places, you are within dimensions of the Matrix.

If you are in the dark space of nothingness after you came out of the body and had an interaction with the beings, you are still in the Matrix simulation and the false presentation of The Void.

If, on the way out of the body, you went through a tunnel of white light, experienced a sensation of flying, and landed in the dark space of nothingness, you are still in the Matrix simulation and the false presentation of The Void.

If you came out of the body and are in the dark space but something or someone else is also there, be that a visual or a voice, you are within dimensions of the Matrix.

If, in any of the above scenarios, you are experiencing "eyes watching you," and it could be anything from multiple random eyes to one big eye, you are still within the astral plane and being interfered with.

Before my Kundalini woke up and my meditative awareness broke out of the astral plane, I saw different types of beings watching me, some reptilian and some not, which made me very uncomfortable to continue my practice. So I asked an old master what to do.

He said, "Stay out of fear and keep going past them. Even if they are watching, they can do nothing to you without your fear of them." After that, I mentally prepared myself before every meditation and trained myself to say: "Yeah. I see you too, whatever..." - and to just keep going past them. After my attitude of indifference towards the "watchers" became strong, I stopped seeing all of it, watching eyes and entities alike.

Quite a few people mentioned that at the beginning of their meditation practice, they saw one big eye looking at them, the same as I did too at the beginning of my practice. I found it strange that so many people were saying the same thing, but back then, I didn't know what it was other than just a big curiosity.

I now think it was the "all-seeing eye" David Icke talks about, but even that goes away as we break out of the Matrix dimensions. All of this interference is for the purpose of scaring you away from continuing with your practice. These entities are trying to stop you because they know you are about to liberate yourself from their system!

All of the above are the common experiences of those who managed to get out of the body but are still learning how to properly navigate their non-physical forms out of the dimensions of the Matrix.

Most people get very excited about their mystical experiences, and although the experiences are a lot of fun and for the first-timers could be life-changing, stopping there would still keep them stuck within dimensions of the Matrix, defeating the purpose of training themselves for the final exit out of the reincarnation system.

If your objective is to exit the system of entrapment, here is what is important to know.

Even if you have had one or more of the experiences I described above, keep training so that you can teach yourself how to properly navigate your non-physical form, direct it where you prefer, and bypass the astral plane and dimensions of the Matrix. This is crucial for your soul liberation.

Be aware that the quantum jump into The True Void is instant. There is no tunnel of white light on the way there; there is no feeling of flying or being "on the way there" at all!

At the beginning of your practice, while you are still paving the way there, when your Kundalini energy rushes up the spine, you might experience a burning sensation in your body, a loud sound inside your mind that only you can hear, and then the sense of explosion inside your head – and then you are gone.

You are in your body doing the Cosmic Cobra Breath in the middle of the night one moment, and the next moment, you are in the Primordial Field, in the Black Ocean of Infinity, the most indescribable state of peace, perfection, and knowing. You are everything, yet you are nowhere to be found.

This is the beginning of your journey to freedom.

PART NINE
When Is It Going to Happen?

So many people write to me with the same exact question: How long does it take to exit the body and experience the True Void? When is this going to happen? Many are ready to give up their practice after trying a few times just because results are not coming "fast enough."

There were also a few who skipped all the information I shared in my workshops and books to prepare their minds for what was to come and went straight to doing rounds and rounds of the Cosmic Cobra Breath, just to find out how unprepared their minds were.

Haste is not the way to do this. Forcing the outcome is not the way to do this either. Getting out of the body and into the True Void is not a race that you need to win and is only the beginning of your journey to freedom.

Keep in mind that we are not training for tomorrow, not even for the next year or two. We are training for the end of our lives, which for most of us is years away.

How long does it take to experience results of your practice? I'm sure it varies from person to person. Some start experiencing different levels of results right away, while for others, it might take months or even years before they dip their toe into the Black Ocean of the Absolute.

I was very "3D" when I started, so it took me three years of consistent daily practice.

When the Matrix-driven voice of the ego that always wants everything "faster" and "more" starts speaking within you, telling you not to even try as three years is too long of a wait; or telling you to quit because the outcome you are working towards isn't happening "fast enough," get a hold of the part of yourself that knows that you've got time.

Keep in mind that one experience of diving into the Absolute is a victory, but it isn't enough for our goal. *We are working towards developing a skill of entering the True Void regularly and at will and being comfortable with doing so.*

Do the practice with curiosity and enjoy it. It will change your life and your state of being, regardless of whether you land in the True Void tomorrow or in a few years. This part I can guarantee.

PART TEN
Where Do We Go after Death?

Another common question that I received all year long was this: if we don't go back to Earth, where do we go? I provided a list of possible options in my first book "LEAVING THE TRAP".

In this book, which is for a more advanced reader, allow me to give you the most optimal answer that I'm aware of today. Only those who have experienced the True Void will understand this.

We go into the Infinite Nowhere, where everything exists at the same time.

We go into nowhere, no time, no form, we return into the primordial field of unlimited consciousness, the very fabric of our souls. We exit the simulation, the Matrix, the entrapment of all sorts, and we become free, infinite, unlimited, and endless.

This is our soul's return back to its True Home, back into the Absolute, back into the unmanifest, back to the very essence of ourselves; and it will very much feel like the Home so many of us long for on the soul level.

We can rest in that indescribable state for as long as we want to, but we won't be Joe Smith or Jane Jones any longer. We will be everything. We will be nothing. We will be all-encompassing, limitless and endless, free from any sort of form, liberated from any restriction, restraint or control.

And if at any point of timelessness an aspect of us decides that it wants to go into form again, we will be free to yet again pull a part of ourselves away from this field and extend a tiny part of our soul fabric into any experience we want. It will be just like a narrow tentacle of an octopus stretched away from its big body.

This choice will be free from anyone else's imposition, be that a simulation, a control mechanism or an entrapment system of any sort.

It will be the choice of the liberated sovereign soul, free to decide for itself what and when it wants to experience.

I'll see you in The Field!

ABOUT THE AUTHOR

Isabella Greene is a Metaphysical Specialist, Spiritual Healer, and best-selling author committed to the evolution of consciousness and the liberation of humanity.

Her debut book, *LEAVING THE TRAP: How to Exit the Reincarnation Cycle*, has garnered widespread attention, leading to appearances on major programs such as Coast-to-Coast AM, Next Level Soul, the JeffMara Podcast, and IckonicTV. She is also featured in the 2024 groundbreaking documentary *The Great Unknown* and David Icke's book *The Reveal*.

Isabella has been exploring the afterlife realm since the age of 17 through astral projection, near-death experiences, and observations at the moments of people's passing. A decade ago, she discovered an ancient yogic technique that enabled her to leave her body at will.

Since then, Isabella has been practicing out-of-body travel that goes beyond the afterlife dimension, liberating the soul from the reincarnation trap.

Today, Isabella shares her knowledge and teaches the practices she has mastered, helping those ready to transform their reality, reclaim soul sovereignty, and escape the cycle of reincarnation at the end of this lifetime.

For more information about Isabella and her work on exiting reincarnation, visit www.TheVoidAcademy.net.

Made in the USA
Las Vegas, NV
26 September 2024

95818898R00111